J

Thanks for your friendship,
inspiration, and all around
grooviness.

— Stanley

IDEA+OLOGY

First published in the United States of America by
Rockport Publishers, a member of
Quayside Publishing Group
100 Cummings Center
Suite 406-L
Beverly, Massachusetts 01915-6101
Telephone: (978) 282-9590
Fax: (978) 283-2742
www.rockpub.com

Library of Congress Cataloging-in-Publication Data
Hainsworth, Stanley.
  Idea-ology : the designer's journey : turning ideas into inspired designs / Stanley Hainsworth.
     p. cm.
  Includes index.
  ISBN-13: 978-1-59253-597-2
  ISBN-10: 1-59253-597-6
  1. Design--History--21st century. 2. Designers--Psychology. I. Title. II. Title: Designer's journey. III. Title:
Turning ideas into inspired designs.
  NK1397.H35 2010
  745.4--dc22

                                                      2009039116
                                                      CIP

ISBN-13: 978-1-59253-597-2
ISBN-10: 1-59253-597-6

10 9 8 7 6 5 4 3 2 1

Design: Tether // Seattle, WA // www.tetherinc.com

Printed in China

IDEA+OLOGY

THE DESIGNER'S JOURNEY: TURNING IDEAS INTO INSPIRED DESIGNS

STANLEY HAINSWORTH

BEVERLY MASSACHUSETTS

ROCKPORT PUBLISHERS

CONTENTS

01 THE DESIGNER'S JOURNEY:
THE SPARK 9

02 THE DESIGNER'S JOURNEY:
THE STRUGGLE 73

03
THE DESIGNER'S JOURNEY:
THE WORK 133

04
THE DESIGNER'S JOURNEY:
THE RESOLUTION 191

INTRODUCTION

BY LOOKING TO THE WORLD OF PERSONAL EXPERIENCES AND DRAWING FROM INSPIRATIONS THAT ARE UNIQUE TO US, WE HAVE AN INSPIRATION POOL THAT NO ONE ELSE CAN REPLICATE.

Writing a book is a long, hard slog, but the rewards are many. Being able to reconnect with the many amazing designers I have met over the years is the main reward. To hear them passionately describe their own creative journeys has inspired me anew.

I have been lucky enough in my career to work with hundreds of designers from all over the world. They all share one thing in common: the desire to do something cool, original, and memorable. But over the past few years, I've increasingly noticed that the well that many designers go to for original ideas comprises annuals, magazines, and the Web. Designers have always been inspired from the work of others. The danger now is that because of the availability of creative work that others

have done, the sole place they get their inspiration is the work of others. There is a difference between inspiration, influence, and imitation.

Inspiration has always been an important part of the designer's journey. Watching and learning from others inspires us to think and create in new ways. Influence happens many times as we work with someone more experienced and we learn from that person, being influenced by his or her way of thinking and expression. But imitation is looking at the work someone else has done and re-creating it with a twist to make it our own. Inspiration and influence is the way we grow and learn as designers. Imitation is taking an unoriginal shortcut and feeding off someone else's inspiration.

If designers look only to each other for inspiration, we will eventually be feeding on ourselves and will turn into an inbred creative family looking increasingly homogenous. We all have a well of creativity that we need to fill. If we fill that well with the work of others, we run the risk of being derivative, as all the inspiration we draw from is derived from others.

We need outside creative inspiration to keep us fresh. And that comes from looking outside our design community and tapping into life. By looking to the world of personal experiences and drawing from inspirations that are unique to us, we have an inspiration pool that no one else can replicate.

I love talking to designers and hearing about what they do outside of work. One is a preacher, many are musicians or fine artists, some are parents, and others race bikes or sing opera or spend many hours on humanitarian causes. All of these outside pursuits are rich areas to mine for inspiration. Bringing your life into your work is a good thing. It will spark ideas that are unique because they come from your unique experiences.

I'm excited to share with you the work of some amazing designers who inspire me. They will take us through their process and how they went from the inspiration that sparked their "idea," through the struggle of making sense of that idea, to the work of sketching and bringing that idea to life, to the refinement and resolution of the final product.

If I've learned one thing from writing this book, it's that inspiration comes from anywhere and everywhere. Although traveling to London, Tokyo, or New York City is certainly inspirational, you can find the inspiration for your design problem by taking a stroll around the block in your hometown. So, after you've read a few pages go out for a walk and keep your eyes wide open. You'll know it when you see it.

Stanley Hainsworth

SECTION
01

THE DESIGNER'S JOURNEY:
THE SPARK

The moment when you're struck by an idea that you think might turn into something, but you don't know where it will take you or how you will get there.

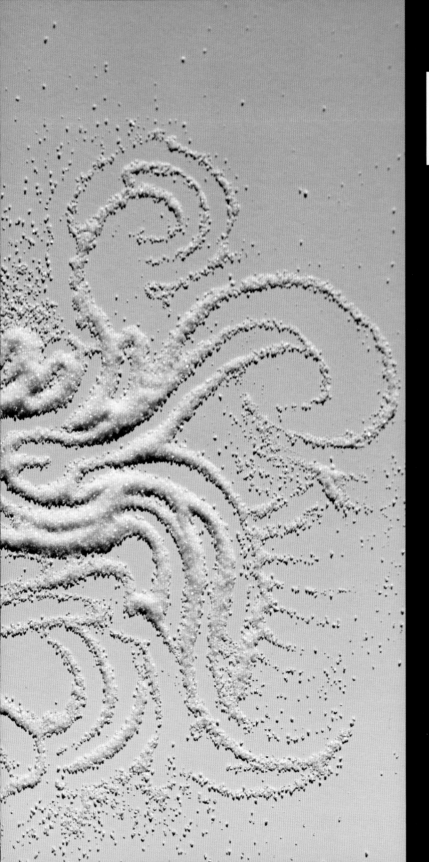

01

GRAPHIC ARTIST
BOWEN ISLAND, BC, CANADA

MARIAN BANTJES

GETS INSPIRED BY BREAKFAST.

In 1994, Marian founded design firm Digitopolis, where she was co-owner and principal designer for nine years until she became a "lapsed graphic designer." Her deep experience in typesetting and design shows in her delightfully hard-to-define work. She is a frequent presenter and writer on design worldwide.

I MOSTLY GET MY INSPIRATION FROM THINGS UNRELATED TO WHAT I DO.

Inspiration can come from anywhere and at any time. There's a difference between inspiration, influence, and reference. When I'm asked what inspires me, I think people expect the answer to be more about a particular reference. For instance, going to a book to see how a certain style looks, that's reference material; going through books or magazines and picking up ideas, that's influence.

For me, inspiration is a spark out of nowhere, a leap of the imagination, often from a surprising source. I mostly get my inspiration from things unrelated to what I do.

It's that moment of juxtaposition when the familiar meets the unfamiliar, the known meets the unknown, and your brain has to connect these things. If we make these inspirational connections, we can create things that spark people's imaginations.

I love cereal. So, I guess I really took the line "play with your food" to heart when I made this piece. I haven't used it yet. What can I say? I'm a huge cereal fan.

I was in Seattle in a toy store, and on the counter was a box with decal sheets for old model airplanes. I picked up a few and put them in an envelope for later reference. Doing something that referenced the decals was on my ideas list for probably seven years. Last year, the Society of Graphic Designers of Canada needed a poster for a sustainability event. They didn't want it to be all green and leafy, so I looked at my list and decided it was time to use the decals.

A lot of my ideas come from wanting to work with particular materials. I'm into fur now. It's showing up in some of my work, like this CalPoly poster I did. The medium can help develop the creative. It kind of speaks to you and inspires you to create what it wants to be.

I'm getting ideas all the time. They come from walking down the street, from watching a movie, from reading. I get a lot of sparks from reading. I'll be reading an article and I'll leap up and write something down. I have more ideas than I can execute. I keep a long "ideas" list that I categorize: film, clothing, graphics, and so on. These vary from grand ideas to little graphic things like "make something with sugar." I used to keep my list of ideas in little notebooks and scraps of paper all over, but now I usually enter them into a text file on my computer. Some of the ideas have been sitting there for years.

When I get a project, I usually have an idea right away or overnight. Sometimes if I'm desperate, I'll hunt through my list for the idea. But it usually pops into my head from some kind of logical or illogical association.

I guess what I do is have this mental and physical storehouse full of thoughts, words, and materials—and I'm always adding to it. I have more ideas than I'll be ever able to use.

....

I always liked playing with sugar at the breakfast table when I was a kid. In fact, I still do it. I made a piece called "Indestructible" for Fox River Paper Company. I, of course, destroyed it by bumping into it. Stefan Sagmeister saw "Indestructible" and wanted something like it. That's when I did "Things I have learned so far in my life." I did six different versions of the same sentence in sugar. I did it without sketches, just freehand on white paper. I just let the sugar do what it wanted to do.

I spend a lot of time thinking. It's really helpful for me. I was reading an article about the need for downtime and getting sleep. About how the time spent sitting around and staring at the sky is really important for people who need to be inspired, because they're always scrambling for ideas. I'm what some would call kind of lazy. I like to just sit and stare at the forest, and that's when I get some of my best ideas.

My best ideas come from the way I live my life. If I feed my life, it will give me ideas when I need them.

I have a number of materials sitting around waiting to be used. For example, I'm collecting dirt from all over the world: South Africa, Bali, Brazil, California. When the time comes, I'll be ready to make something with the dirt. I have burgeoning collections of things that I can't wait to use.

STEFAN BUCHER

IS A MAN POSSESSED WITH IDEAS.

When an idea pops into Stefan G. Bucher's head, he can't stop until he somehow makes it real. Over the years, this has led him to move from his native Germany to southern California to become the man behind the 344 Design empire. He has designed CD covers for just about every major record company, and has since moved on to making books and art catalogs. He's good at it, too. He received the British Design & Art Direction Yellow Pencil Award and was included in the 2004 Art Directors Young Guns. He is now the man behind the Daily Monster at www.dailymonster.com.

DO THAT WHICH IS CLOSE TO YOUR HEART. IT'S AN EXPRESSION OF WHAT YOU LOVE IN LIFE, AND OTHERS WILL RECOGNIZE THAT.

There are so many ways to get inspired; to feed yourself. No one is looking through design annuals ripping people off because they're lazy or mean. It just feels comfortable. Designers, like all humans, want to run with the tribe on some level. You stick with the family by copying the behavior and work of others. You align yourself. You calibrate. You get comfortable and efficient. By looking at annuals, you figure out what you need to do to get into annuals, but if you want to evolve your own work, looking at annuals is a dead end, of course.

I don't really switch off inspiration anymore. I've broken down the barrier between me and what surrounds me. Everything is editable. I crop my environment, looking at everything as a Photoshop source and a retouching opportunity. I take photos when I can, but there are times when I force myself not to take notes or photos, so I have to truly remember. Otherwise, I start remembering the photos and wipe out the memory of the experience in the process.

Back in 1999, I started designing and illustrating flyers for bossa:nova, Jason Bentley's weekly club night here in Los Angeles. My friend Jennifer Stone was in charge of that, and handed me a flyer to one of the shows—Kruder & Dorfmeister. I said, "Could I please redo your fliers, just as kind of a humanitarian type gesture? They can't stay like this."

When it comes to pursuing new ideas in my work, I have a factory showroom model theory. No client wants to be the first to buy anything. They all want to be the second—after someone else already worked out the kinks. You have to have at least one produced example to show that it won't blow up, that you know how to get it done.

Graphic design and illustration are all about taking control of a little piece of the world and making it look exactly as you would want it to be, and the fliers I created for bossa:nova were one of the first times I was really able to do that. I did dozens of them for about five years.

Around the same time, I started making the flower posters for New Year's. These were projects I created for myself as the client; they were my R&D department and my showroom models so that I could go to a potential paying client and say, "You like these? I'd like to do something like this for you." Start doing what you want to do so that you can get the kind of work you want.

It's like this for me; the responsible thing is to do that which is close to your heart. It's an expression of what you love in life, and others will recognize that. They'll say, "I understand how this feels for you. I do something different, but that's how it feels for me, too." And they just want to be a part of it.

01

don't plan what I'm going to do,
plan the method and then let
the thing become what it wants
to become. I have the tools to
facilitate that process.

02

When I start, I don't know what the
drawing or the monster will look like
or what the story will be. I discover
it as I go along.

03

The story comes totally out of the
shape each monster chooses to
assume. The Christmas monster has
this huge beak, which means that
it probably has a loud, strange bird
voice. Everything flows from that.

04

After the timelapse drawing is
finished and the Holiday Monster
walks off the paper and out of
frame, we fade to black and enter
a new scene. A monster hand
knocks on a festively decorated door.

05

The door opens and reveals three
caroling monsters. They launch
into a spirited version of "Deck
the Halls." It's clear that they've
practiced hard. They're very good
singers with sweet voices.

06

Suddenly, our Holiday Monster walks
into the scene. It decides to join in
the fun and begins to sing along—
loudly and badly. It has the heart of
Pavarotti and the voice of a wounded
goose. The carol is ruined. The other
monsters are not happy, as the door
slams in their face.

07

They angrily tell the poor Holiday
Monster to get lost …

08

The Holiday Monster is sad. It meant
no harm. It just wanted to sing along
with the others. It hangs its head
and moves back. It doesn't want to
cause trouble.

09

The other monsters go on to the next house. They knock and get ready to try again.

When the door opens they start into "Jingle Bells." All is well and they're sounding better than ever. The Holiday Monster looks on from a distance.

10

He simply can't resist the music. It just has to join in. And it does. And it's awful. Pee Wee Herman after a botched tracheotomy would sound better than this. Another door is slammed shut, and the caroling monsters are getting seriously ticked off. They decide to take action.

11

The Scarf Monster produces a long rope …

12

… as Red Sweater and Turtleneck make for the Holiday Monster. They grab his beak and get to work. As the screen fades to black, we hear the sounds of a struggle.

3

When the dust … well, when the snow settles, the Holiday Monster realizes what happened. The others have tied up its beak. It struggles to free itself, but its arms are too short. It gives up and starts crying— heaving with big honking sobs of disappointment and despair.

14

But just when things are at their bleakest, as it hears itself sob, inspiration strikes! We fade to black.

15

As the picture fades back up, the Holiday Monster's beak knocks on another door. The door opens …

16

… and the Holiday Monster bursts into a brilliant, jazzy version of "Jingle Bells" using its expanding and retracting beak like a trombone. It always knew that it loved making music. It just hadn't figured out the right way to make it yet. The monster grins proudly and takes a bow. The End.

The whole thing becomes easier when I do quirkier work. As soon as you commit to putting out work that's personal to you, you start meeting people who do their own thing. It becomes a feedback loop. They start letting you in on interesting things that allow you to make more interesting things that inspire them. Once that kicks in, you'll have so many opportunities to work that you can start being selective and be conscious of what you want your work to be.

I started out as an illustrator in Germany. I did everything by hand. Then I went to Art Center College of Design and got a computer. I could finally do the straight lines, smooth gradations, and crisp type I always tried to do by hand while growing up. After a few years of that, I realized I was hiding behind the method—the technique

was a hedge. I got to the point where I said, "It's time to put my own handwriting back into this."

Daily Monsters came at a time when I really needed a creative outlet. The technique was surprisingly conscious—it came out of one of the New Year's posters. The first poster out of that series was "344 Flowers." At first, I used cocktail straws to blow the ink to create the technique, but I got a tremendous headache almost immediately, so I switched to pressurized canned air. The compressed air opened the door to those fantastic shapes. So, you see, I can depend on something other than my brain. The story came from the drawing. When you really have to start from scratch all your anxieties and fears come into it. But the blot gives me a start, and I can relax into my method.

It's like music: You do years and years of scales so that you can start improvising. Design is improvisation. Modern design education wants to be cool, so it skips the scales and takes you straight to improvisation, because that's the fun part! But it doesn't work that way. The one thing that's missing from almost every single portfolio I see is the ability to set type beautifully. You can't get to the fun stuff without rigor. Skills come first. You have to know your craft at the body level.

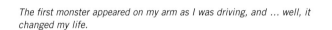

The first monster appeared on my arm as I was driving, and ... well, it changed my life.

03

NIKE
BEAVERTON, OR, USA

GREG HOFFMAN

IS ALL ABOUT JUXTAPOSITION.

Greg Hoffman is vice president of Global Brand Design at Nike Inc., with design groups in Portland, Oregon, the Netherlands, Shanghai, and Tokyo. Greg leads the team in building Nike's brand identity, brand communication, and brand experience through a variety of design mediums, including product, graphic, environmental, and digital. His work encompasses projects ranging from Nike's World Cup and Olympic consumer experiences to Nike flagship retail venues and brand identities for Nike's athletes and teams.

BE INSPIRED BY THE PAST TO CREATE A RICH AND SOULFUL FUTURE.

I get inspired by getting outside. Meeting new people, traveling to new places, and immersing myself in new experiences is essential to finding inspiration. Spending time in different cities throughout the world allows me access to different cultures and approaches to design. These diverse experiences help to serve as catalysts during the creative process and ensure that the design work represents a world beyond just my daily experiences.

Cataloging and documenting these trips is key to getting the most out of them. And technology has made that process easier, not only to gather but also to share. What used to require stacks of paper, magazines, slides, videos, and so on now fills a multigigabyte hard drive. The hard drive becomes an inventory of inspiration that you can continually draw upon.

Besides drawing inspiration from what is new and emerging, I find that having an understanding and appreciation for design history and the design movements of the past is just as essential to me. So, you could say I have two buckets of inspiration: past and present. These two visual catalogs represent fashion, architecture, print, brand identity, film, and other design mediums. Having all of

this great reference material is a good starting point, but it's what you do with it that counts.

Drawing upon the past and the present for design inspiration, and then applying them both in the design process, can lead to some of the most interesting innovations. I like to think about it as presenting the past in a modern context or applying a contemporary motif to a timeless form. It's really about that juxtaposition; that mashup. It's the relationship between the past and present, which ultimately leads to something inspirational and innovative.

This approach can work whether I'm designing a uniform for the Brazilian national football team, creating a new environment devoted to customization, or designing a logo for an athlete. This provides the consumer (or the athlete) with a design solution that has hints of familiarity but is undeniably contemporary in its form and function. It's an approach that allows us to remain true to our athletic heritage while reshaping the definition of sport—the future of sport.

....

We hired sculptors to add to the body scan forms and bring out all the unique characteristics of the athlete, whether it was Kobe Bryant or LeBron James, and we got a life-size, realistic-looking sculpture. Then we could copy and create as many Kobes or LeBrons as we wanted. Instead of something more typical, like photography, this allowed us to present the athlete in a way that consumers could interact with and compare themselves to.

In terms of global reach and how many different aspects and consumer experiences existed with a project, one of the biggest initiatives we've taken on is designing for the Beijing 2008 Olympics. Every four years, you need to bring something fresh to the market. We're always trying to bring the athlete closer to the consumer—up close and personal, if you will.

For the Olympics, we thought about how to take that idea of the heroic sculpture, but to do it based on a specific moment at the games. How do you create that in a unique and memorable way, and let that anchor some of these consumer experiences that we do?

We worked with a team in Los Angeles and did body scans of the athletes. From the body scans, we created a three-dimensional print of each athlete, creating a form, like when Liu Xiang goes over a hurdle or Asafa Powell explodes out of the blocks.

That's just a sliver of one of the many things we did for the Beijing Games, combining all design mediums around that initiative—photography, print, consumer experiences, and so on.

We placed the life-sized realistic-looking sculptures in China, Europe, and in the U.S. Imagine the difference for the consumer, used to the traditional department store mannequin, being able to see an extremely realistic, dynamic version of Liu Xiang sprinting past you.

The idea of customizing your own shoe with Nike ID has been out there for some time, but the reality is that only a small segment of consumers actually knew what Nike ID was. The more we thought about it, the more it seemed that in order to spark this idea of customization, we needed to bring consumers into a 3-D experience.

We started to play around with this idea of a physical design studio—Nike ID Studio—that was a celebration of the creativity people have within themselves. The inspiration comes from the product design. We integrated those elements into the architecture and the visual language of the spaces, essentially coding the spaces.

We looked back to the craftsmanship of seventeenth- and eighteenth-century artisans—burning patterns into wood, and then filling those patterns with heated gold, creating a beautiful design. Taking inspiration from that, we created athlete line-work collages and burned them into table surfaces using some of the Old World techniques. Being inspired by some of the techniques from the past allowed us to touch the romance and edge of what those artists did. Drawing from those practices, but putting them through our filter, we ended up with this beautiful, modern aesthetic that was really soulful and inspirational. It was inspirational to people who love footwear and people who just wanted to be in a creative space.

We looked at Victorian wallpaper and how ornate and detailed it was, and said, "What if we did elaborate wallpaper, but it was made up entirely of different iconic shoe designs?" So, at first glance, you might not get it, but the more time you spend within the space, the more details you pick up.

For the ID London cube, we wanted the product itself to become an element of the architecture. This two-story glass cube we created allowed us to display more than 1,000 pairs of footwear. It creates a huge visual impact from outside, and upon entering the cube, it helps deliver a complete product-customization experience.

Many of the things within the Nike ID London cube experience celebrate innovation and technology, but we surrounded that experience with handcrafted art and patterns. Looking back, some of the designs created by Old World craftsmen actually feel more contemporary than designs that use the latest programs and applications. It's great that we have all this technology that enables the design process, but it's how it's used that's important. In this case, technology simply allowed us to refine and enhance design methods that have been around for ages.

Our first Nike ID studio was an intimate 400 square-foot (37 m²) space at 255 Elizabeth Street in New York City, which was followed by a second one in Niketown, New York. But, ultimately, this concept really came to life in London. From a pure environmental design standpoint, it's created a lot of buzz within the design community. But the reality is, if we're receiving a lot of accolades but not delivering a rich and compelling experience to the consumer, who really cares?

In all three of these instances, there was very little compromise in terms of going from inspiration to reality. It's taking the best of what we do—providing product innovation for athletes—and presenting it through an inspirational and dynamic expression.

HATCH DESIGN
SAN FRANCISCO, CA, USA

KATIE JAIN +
JOEL TEMPLIN

ARE DRIVEN BY NEAR PERFECTION.

Joel Templin and Katie Jain founded Hatch Design in 2007. Since then, they've attracted great clients and have gained critical acclaim for their design and branding work. But this new entity, Hatch, was born to enable them to do more than help clients build brands; it was designed to allow them to create and grow their own brands, as well. JAQK Cellars is the first idea to crack out of the egg, and it couldn't be a more beloved first hatchling.

WHEN YOU'RE LOOKING FOR IDEAS, IT'S IMPORTANT THAT YOU GO SOMEPLACE TOTALLY RANDOM.

JT: Inspiration comes from so many places. We never go to design annuals for inspiration. We'll look at old annuals from the 1940s or 1950s for reference because we are attracted to that craft sensibility.

KJ: We have a cool library that we reference every day.

JT: Starting a project is an organic process. We start with everyone pulling scrap imagery and talking about it. Everyone chimes in with several sets of eyes looking at things. Some happy accidents happen along the way. It's an "if they're zigging, we're zagging" kind of thing.

KJ: It's like we put up the pages from the design annuals and say, "Don't do this. Let's do something new." The things from our collections are from places like the bookstores in Japantown in San Francisco, where we look at imported product packaging to get a good range of ideas and get inspired. Then we start looking at everything as a collective and start grouping things together to see a potential path that the project might take.

JT: It's important that you go someplace totally random. Say you're doing beauty packaging, and you look at those security patterns from the inside of envelopes for inspiration, and they end up on the packaging for a high-end skin care product. When you juxtapose things and objects in an unexpected way, you end up with unexpected results.

KJ: We started the wine project, where we created the identity and packaging, as a creative outlet for ourselves and our designers so that we could have complete control over the project. We didn't have to go through focus groups or be second-guessed by multilayered corporations. We had ultimate creative control over every single touch point. It was a dream to design our own thing. Because we were 100 percent committed to every little thing it has become an important case study for other client work. The product is successful and is taking off and becoming a great self-promotion for Hatch.

....

JT: We have 140 drawers from an old hardware store. Each drawer contains one to three found objects: canceled checks, stock certificates, old packaging, old fishing lures, old matchbooks, a mixed bag of anything and everything. When we travel, we always hit up antique stores or flea markets to add to our collections.

JT: The wine project started a long time ago while I was having lunch with a friend. My friend's uncle was a wine distributor and I was looking for something new to work on. He said we could buy 100 cases of wine, and we could design the label and his uncle would distribute the wine. Because his uncle was in Nevada, we said we could call it Snake Eyes or something that related to casinos and gambling. That idea passed with time, but then we started Hatch and we brought it up again. We started brainstorming names like High Rollers, Snake Eyes, Full House, and Royal Flush.

KJ: Then we thought, let's put a card on a bottle of white wine so that you can see the back of it through the bottle. We wanted to create our own products and that was the vision when we started Hatch, but it's tough to find the right product. We got so fired up about this wine. We decided that maybe we were on to something.

Then we partnered with a phenomenal winemaker. It took us to a whole new level where the quality of the wine stands on its own, and when paired with the packaging, it made it really successful.

JT: We were going to call our new wine concept High Roller, but then we brought in a writer and he came up with the name JAQK. It was a higher idea of Jack/Ace/Queen/King. It evolved into JAQK Cellars, and the creative started evolving from there.

KJ: It's an interesting market. We've done a lot of work in the wine industry over the years, and we've realized how little the big companies spend on brand. We saw the opportunity when we started this because we were just donating our time to our company.

KJ: Through research, we found out how huge poker is— 80 million Americans go to Las Vegas every year. We were inspired by the storytelling and tradition of gaming and wanted to incorporate that into our designs.

JT: In the wine industry, it's all about what's in the bottle. We almost did too good a job with the packaging because of how beautiful it is. Everyone was used to what exists in the industry, so when they saw this beautiful packaging, they thought it might be a gimmick or a novelty.

JT: Even our business cards are minted metal poker chips. When we give our cards out to people they say, "Can I keep it?" and we say yes, and then they say, "Thank you." How often does that happen to you?

JT: As designers, and because we are our own clients, we'll always be able to evolve the design and do anything we want. For example, we decided we wanted to incorporate real poker chips into the design of our labels, so we did. We even had a custom jig made so that someone could screen-print the poker chips by hand.

KJ: We invited our friends to the warehouse and offered them some wine in one hand and a glue gun in the other hand, and we had a party gluing poker chips to the bottles.

JT: We used top-of-the-line foil and cork. We stamped the end of the cork with different messages so that you have a little surprise when you open the bottle.

KJ: The goal for this company is to prove that you can have high-quality, fine wine and playful, interesting packaging at the same time. People enjoy it before they drink it and enjoy it even more after they try it.

JT: We've had tastings, and afterward people ask if they can take the empty bottles home with them. People don't want to throw them away. Our opportunities for the future are very exciting with line extensions that could make it bigger than just wine.

05

JAGER DI PAOLA KEMP (JDK) DESIGN
BURLINGTON, VT, USA

MICHAEL JAGER

TAKES INSPIRATION HEAD-ON.

For twenty years, Michael Jager has directed the multidisciplinary efforts of a design studio whose process is informed by emotional, rational, and cultural forces and whose focus centers on the idea that design distinction matters. His collaborative output for a multitude of today's most important and relevant brands is recognized worldwide by design periodicals, books, competitions, exhibitions, and his peers. Michael lives in Vermont with his wife and partner, Giovanna, and their three children.

I FIND INSPIRATION IN THE DETAILS, THE TEXTURE, THE RHYTHM, THE PLACE.

From my experience, the creative process never sleeps. I process experiences and memories differently than so-called left-brained thinkers who need to rationalize everything. Maybe it's because I was awful at math in high school, but fortunately I was okay at drawing. I was always trying to do album covers or movie posters, anything other than math.

I can remember images, color, type, textures, and experiences more deeply than something like math. If I'm trying to solve something, I may go for a run, go for a walk down a New York City street, or go to a store or a restaurant and find some inspiration in the details, the texture, the rhythm, the place. I suppose it comes down to how willing you are to be open-minded about what something might represent or communicate.

A few years ago, I went to Portugal at the end of the summer. I stayed at my brother-in-law's home near the beach in the southern part of Portugal. I'd never been there before. I spent a lot of time looking around in the little village and noticed bullfighting posters around town.

We watched one of the Portuguese bullfights on TV, and it was kind of like seeing an NFL football game here, or a soccer game in the UK. It started with an equestrian riding segment with a rider poking and provoking the bull for about fifteen minutes to get him excited and emotionally charged. Then an individual called a forcado comes out leading a group of men. He's wearing traditional matador-type gear.

It's all about the respect of the bull and the family's respect and responsibility to the bull. It is bloody and scary and gnarly and beautiful, all at once. The forcado takes on the role of taunting the bull and then getting his respect with the help of his trusted partners.

Magnified by the energy of the TV experience, the drawing, and seeing the posters for the real events in the local area my interest started to spin. When we finally got the chance to see a bullfight in person, my 16-year-old son and I went to a little town called Albufeira. The event starts late at night and the location is the equivalent of a rural California stock car race track. We saw people being carried out in stretchers at midnight. It was all so punk rock, and raw, and surreally beautiful.

I started noticing these posters of bullfights and traveling circuses. These local ranches were presenting these bullfights. My relative explained the difference between bullfighting in Portugal and in Spain. In Portugal, you don't kill the bull—it's more an equestrian relationship and experience overall, though there is blood, as I soon discovered.

The forcado is usually one of the sons of the family that owns the bull. He's there with his friends or cousins or brothers. The forcado stands head-on, staring down the bull from across the arena, yelling "Toro, toro, toro" as he steps closer and closer. The bull, of course, is getting revved up and pawing at the ground. Very classic, very raw and real; the power and intensity are actually quite scary.

Behind the forcado is his relative or friend, and then another friend 10 feet (3 m) behind, and then another one 10 feet (3 m) behind him. A pack of the men are gathered behind the last person. The forcado's goal is to get the bull to charge him head-on. The bull rushes the forcado and slams him against the person behind him, and he slams into the next person behind him, until the bull hits the group of men, who all try to harness the incredible energy of the bull.

I went to the beach the day after the bullfight and continued drawing. At that point, my sketchpads were filled with images of bulls and forcados. When I returned home, I had to prepare for the annual JDK Design summer staff meeting, which is a daylong event. I always do a presentation about where we're going as a company. I had an idea about the importance of collaboration in multidisciplinary design and what this meant to JDK. I wanted to get the point across that we should be as masterful as we can at making the experience of design inspiring and that we're respecting all the people that it takes to create a successful design project. The account person is as important as the designer, as is the production person, as is the client. When a project is really beautiful, it's because of that harmonic relationship with all those parts.

That was when the sketches of the bulls and the bullfight came into my mind, with the metaphor being the forcado and the supporting group. The design process is the controlling of this wild beast by the forcado and his comrades. It's all these people working together with their comrades in trying to solve a complex design problem. I saw this as a metaphor for collaboration and trying to come up with powerful ideas together.

I told my team about Portuguese bullfighting and how the forcado and his team worked and how it all related to collaboration. The response was exciting, but risky and scary for me. As creative director, I'm supposed to inspire these eighty-five people, so I wanted to make a point about collaboration that was memorable. I wanted to put myself into a scary, creative position that then harmonized our studio's energy.

This whole journey went from a trip to Portugal and images of bulls on TV and on street posters, to drawings on the beach with my children, to a midnight bullfight. It was this multidimensional catalog of ideas and images that ended up becoming the catalyst to memorably communicate something that I thought was important and useful to our design culture.

After seeing this bullfight on television, I was at the beach with my kids drawing on the sand and I started drawing bulls, and I was thinking of Picasso's bulls and the imagery I'd just experienced. Then my kids joined in and we were drawing bull families.

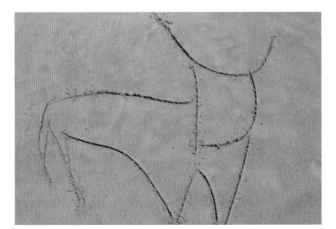

While I was taking the team through this concept, I had two pieces of plywood that were attached with hinges. While I was talking, I took buckets of paint, a mop, and a rag and I painted a gigantic piece of art that was 8 feet square (5.8 sq. m). To everyone around me, it looked like an abstract in black, white, red, and gray.

At the end, I explained what a forcado was and related it to facing complex design ideas, and then I stood up the panels and there appeared an 8-foot (2.44 m) high portrait of a bull facing you head-on. No one knew what it was going to be, so everyone was surprised when they saw the painting.

Now when you walk into our studio space, the first thing you see is the painting of the bull's head, reminding everyone who is involved in the creative process to fearlessly approach design and creativity head-on and to remember that inspiration is a beautiful journey.

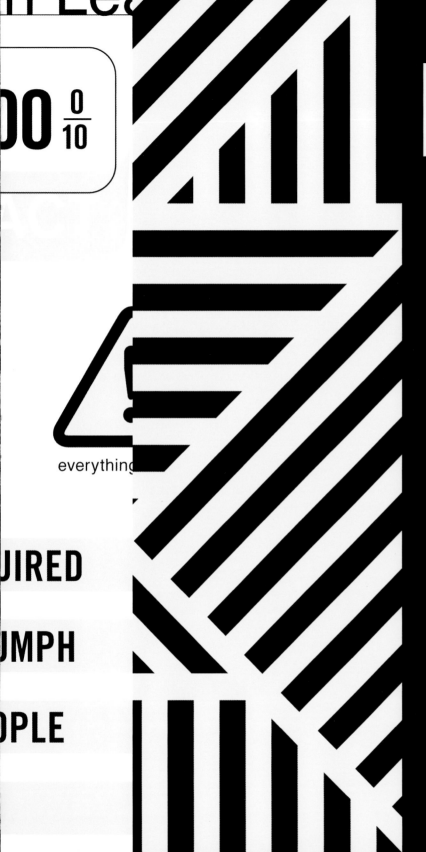

06

MINE
SAN FRANCISCO, CA, USA

CHRISTOPHER SIMMONS

DESIGN HAS CHANGED HIS LIFE. LIFE HAS CHANGED HIS DESIGN.

Christopher Simmons is a Canadian-born, San Francisco–based graphic designer, writer, and educator. He is the author of three books on graphic design and a frequent speaker on graphic design at schools and design organizations across the United States. He has contributed to works in the permanent collections of the San Francisco Museum of Modern Art and the Smithsonian Institution. He is an instructor of design at the California College of Arts in San Francisco (his alma mater), and he runs the design firm, MINE.

THE QUESTION I'M USUALLY TRYING TO ANSWER HAS BEEN ANSWERED COUNTLESS TIMES BY OTHER PEOPLE IN DIFFERENT WAYS.

Someone famously observed that no matter what pathway you make in a park, people will inevitably cut their own paths. So, the way to design a park is to make one pathway and then go back later and look where the grass has been trodden down and cut new paths accordingly.

It's easy to understand this as inspiration or as a metaphor for user interaction on a website or a mobile device, but for me, it's a kind of abstract observation that can really illuminate and locate the notion of a "pure idea." It's a very different experience than approaching problems the way most of us were trained. It's not a formal engagement; it's a conceptual engagement. I carry two Moleskines with me most of the time, but I don't refer to them a lot, because the process of recording something is what lodges it in my brain. It all depends on the time frame—sometimes, I have to draw on my bank of inspiration.

I always start a project by trying to understand the context and scope, and then I try to articulate it back to the client. Sometimes, I get it wrong—which is half of the point; then we can have a dialogue about the nuances so that I can more fully understand the problem we're trying to crack. You could think of that conversation as a kind of path-building exercise. After that, I try not to think about the project for a week (if I have that luxury). The benefit there is that as I walk around and talk or watch a movie or interact with my environment, I start seeing that the question I'm trying to answer has been answered countless times by countless other people in countless different ways. Understanding how those

answers respond to the specifics of different situations—how they differ and how they're the same—is often what helps the pure idea present itself. Sometimes, though, that idea isn't revealed until after the damn thing is designed.

In 2004, we wanted to do a self-promotion for the studio. It was around the time of Bush's reelection, and we wanted to make a political statement against that outcome. At first, we thought it would be funny to do a poster with a big screw and a big bush.

This was our attempt at making a political statement in a self-promotion, but we thought better of it and didn't end up doing it.

NOVEMBER 2

As we were thinking about doing the "Screw Bush" poster, one of the people in our studio was diagnosed with cancer, and we had bigger issues to think about. It shifted our perspective. That's when we started looking at a concept that dealt with providing resources to people, rather than just complaining about stuff. We flipped from reacting with a negative political message to generating something much more positive. As we were following this concept, we kept being reminded that there is so much other stuff that isn't right in the world, and we started feeling kind of hopeless. It was then that we came up with the phrase, "Everything is okay." It's a reassuring phrase in one way, but when you scratch a little deeper, you realize that really nothing is okay, and somehow we've all become okay with that. It has a kind of built-in, cyclical cynicism to it that intrigued me.

Of course, like a lot of self-generated projects, it didn't really go anywhere. We sat on the idea for about a year without doing anything, before finally deciding to pull the trigger and build the "Everything is OK" website. It was a meandering process where life events and things that matter to us shaped the direction of the statement we wanted to make. From concept to completion, the whole thing was about an eighteen-month process, but once we solidified the idea, the execution came very rapidly.

Our next task was to promote the site. Naturally, we started thinking about a promotional poster because, after all, designers love making posters. Then something interesting happened. You've heard the joke: How many designers does it take to change a lightbulb? (Answer: Does it have to be a lightbulb?) We finally asked ourselves, "Does it have to be a poster?" and that's when we came up with the idea of placing the statement "Everything is OK" on caution tape.

The point of the caution tape was to drive people to the website—kind of like a guerilla marketing campaign. It was really just intended as an artifact connected to a bigger idea. We found that people were much more interested in the expression and the artifact than in engaging with these monumental causes. In other words, people didn't care about the site, but were emailing, asking for "that cool tape." We were resistant at first, since it felt like selling out or cheapening the idea. But people want what they want. You can't force them to walk down a path if it's not taking them where they want to go. So now, that's what the project has become.

Much of the success of "Everything is OK" depends on its neutrality. Although we have our own political, social, cultural, and ethical opinions, we want to make sure we're giving people tools to express their views, not just ours.

People can buy kits of the tape, postcards, and stickers and use those tools to modify spaces, magazines, packaging, and so on. I guess you could say it's become a kind of graphic activist kit.

We have a gallery where people can submit photos of what they've done with the tape or stickers. People have used the tape as the basis for high school pranks and as the foundation of their college thesis. An event organizer contacted us about using it as a wayfinding system for a massive street fair in Toronto.

So, what was initially a medium to promote a message has become the message. It's really become its own idea. We thought we started out with a good idea, but it clearly had imperfections, and we didn't recognize the heart of it. Once we put it into action, the actions of other people revealed the pure idea. You could say it was a form of prototyping, even though that wasn't the plan.

This self-generated project has brought us some attention, but more interesting than that is all the interesting people it has brought us into contact with. I got an email from someone in New York City who saw it on the street. He tracked us down on the Web and said, "I saw this tape on the street and would like that kind of thinking applied to a project I'm working on." It turns out that he's the head of a major international policy think tank in Beijing. Now he wants MINE to work on a project with him. If it wasn't for the authenticity of the project, if it wasn't for the purity of the idea, we would never have connected. In a way, this project has been about the meandering paths that connect us—through ideas—to interesting people with their own interesting problems.

That takes us back to those paths in the park—we learn not through planning and thinking, but by doing, observing, and adapting.

The design agency Landor used 1,000 feet (304.8 m) of the tape for a recent studio event, and it's going up in Taiwan as part of the city's Design Week. The tape has been in group shows at galleries in New York and Chicago, and was recently shown at the Museum of Contemporary Art in Hiroshima, Japan. It even inspired a techno album in Britain. We've sold or given away more than 20,000 feet (6,096 m) of it to people who've used it in any manner of individual and imaginative ways.

everything is ok
everythingisok.com

07

ILLUSTRATOR
BUENOS AIRES, ARGENTINA /
NEW YORK CITY, NY, USA

FERNANDA COHEN

IS INSPIRED BY WATCHING PEOPLE.

Fernanda Cohen grew up in Buenos Aires, Argentina, and splits her time between her home country and New York City, where she has her studio. Besides her illustrations for editorial and corporate clients, she has a line of illustrated kitchenware, notebooks, handbags, and tea towels. She is a teacher at the School of Visual Arts and a writer.

YOUR BRAIN IS A VERY PLIABLE AND ERASABLE SURFACE.

I love watching people at cafés and overhearing conversations. I'm inspired by patterns that I see a lot in architecture. The worst thing for me is to be inspired by other people's work. I don't have other artists' work on my wall. I am inspired by real things, by photographs, by people, by things outside the art world.

I write down a lot of notes in my Moleskine sketchbook—phrases and sentences that will later trigger a thought or a source of inspiration. I sketch a lot in my head when I have an idea. My head is a very pliable and erasable surface—if an idea in my mind is too cliché, I'll edit it until I get something that works and then I'll write it down in words. Later, I will sketch what was in my head and written in my sketchbook, and that's usually very close to what the client will see.

*The Food Affair series came from an idea I had about fat people eating.
This was a personal project that I sent into competitions and used as
mailers that ended up getting me a lot of work, including, I found out
later, my first cover for* The New Yorker *magazine.*

I'm always coming up with ideas, and I'm always drawing and teaching and immersed in my work. I think that because my work and personal lives are one and the same, I draw from everything I encounter for inspiration.

Because I think in words, it's easier to come up with ideas. I take careful notes when listening to a client because certain words will guide me in a direction.

When I think of a good idea I have to execute it. There are times when I write down a good idea and I don't have the time to execute it and I get frustrated. So, if I come up with a great idea I just sketch it. I create my own work a lot from those ideas. My personal work has generated all of my commercial work.

I submitted "Honor Thy Broccoli" to the Step Inside Design 100 competition, and one of the jurors was quoted as liking my piece. I sent her a note thanking her for saying nice things. A few months later, she called me. She said she had a client, Ikram, in Chicago, that wanted to do a series of mailers and she was inspired by the piece I did about the kids and the broccoli. Ikram was one of the first clients to give me a shot.

I had submitted my work to a magazine where you needed to submit three different series. I submitted my Ikram series, Food Affair series, and Funny Petit series.

I came up with the Ikram concept idea in the shower. It just came to me. I get a lot of my ideas in the shower. And if not there, then on an afternoon walk.

I did a personal piece with kids holding up broccoli that says, "Honor Thy Broccoli." This came from a dream I had about how all kids are supposed to hate broccoli. I did pieces like this all day long, and they eventually got me work.

I started taking pictures of myself, and by the end of my time working on the "Honor Thy Clothes" campaign I had three or four hundred pictures, and that's what these illustrations are based on.

The only brief I had said to do a series of mailers based on "Honor Thy Broccoli." So, I changed it to "Honor Thy Clothes." I drew one girl each month in the piece of clothing she wanted me to highlight. They were all naked except for wearing the featured clothing item.

08

ILLUSTRATOR AND DESIGNER
MEXICO CITY, MEXICO

JORGE ALDERETE

GETS INSPIRED BY HIS FRIENDS.

Jorge Alderete is a pop illustrator, influenced by trash culture, 1950s science fiction movies, wrestling, and surf music. His illustrations, animations, and comics have appeared around the world. He graduated with a degree in fine arts from Universidad Nacional de la Plata, Argentina, as a designer in visual communication. He has done animations for MTV Latin America and Japan, and Nickelodeon Latin America and Brazil, and he was the animation de-partment coordinator of MTV Latin America.

MOST OF MY INSPIRATION IS FROM JUST LIVING.

WWW.BLACKCATBONES.ORG

♥ ideal
Conalosa

Libreta No.20 KFT

This is my soft-cover Moleskine that I carry around with notes of things that I see, places I go, and just stuff.

My work is a mix of the city, the street, real things that I see, and fantasy things like monster movies. But most of my inspiration is from just living. I work across all mediums—toys, posters, books, CDs, I even illustrated a football for the NFL experience. I am a creator of fantasies. I indulge in those fantasies with my own design store and gallery.

I started to think about my ten years in Mexico City and my friends, and I wanted to celebrate. Maybe I could do an exhibition, a movie, a documentary, a poster, or even a book—I wasn't sure. But I was thinking about the concept, not the product. It wasn't until later that I would figure out what the best thing would be. The inspiration for this project would be my friends and our experiences.

Sometimes, I just scan these small drawings and make a poster. I try to go everywhere with this sketchbook. I never know when I'm going to see something and get an idea.

Maybe I'll be in the subway and see or think of something. So, I make a fast sketch in my book. You never know where or when an idea will come to you.

This is the first time I've drawn real people. On this project, I moved toward making fantasy characters out of my friends where I mixed reality and fantasy. All of my work generally is moving from fantasy to reality, and this time it was moving from reality with a small mix of fantasy. I went everywhere with my Moleskine and my camera. I met my friends casually, without an appointment, and I went to places where I thought I could find friends I haven't seen in years.

This was a personal project, and I didn't even think about making any money from it. I just wanted to reconnect with the forty-four people in the book, but instead of throwing a party, I created a book that celebrated my friends.

I was lucky in that I found a French publisher that liked the idea of the rock scene, the underground, and the clubs in Mexico City. I didn't have to change anything. They understood the concept of the book and gave me total freedom.

When I was working out the book in my head, I started to think as the book characters would think. When I remembered something from one of them, I tried to put something in my sketchbook. Some of the first drafts of the drawings are in pencil and some are in paint.

When I found my friends, I talked to them and took a picture. I took notes while I talked to them. The most difficult part was writing about the people, because I naturally draw to put down my thoughts.

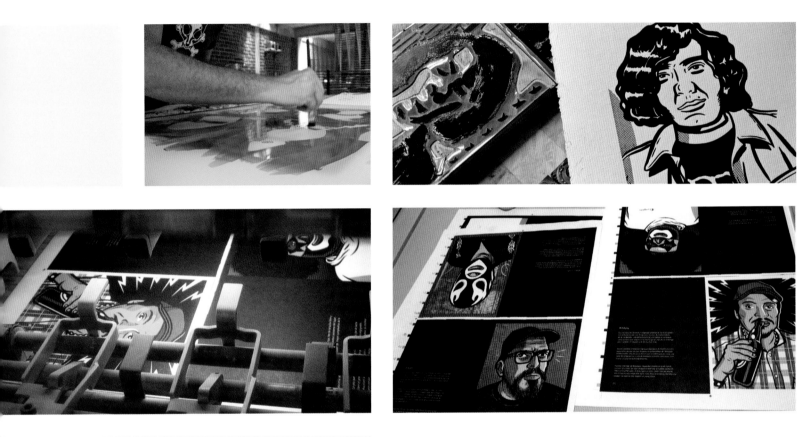

I was able to silkscreen and letterpress posters and T-shirts from the book images as well.

The book was printed in Mexico City, so I could be there for each step, including the printing and distribution of the book.

I'm very happy with the finished book because I was able to take it from the beginning to the end, each step along the way.

THE SPARK REDUX

ALONG THE DESIGN JOURNEY THERE ARE SO MANY WAYS TO HELP IGNITE INSPIRATION. THE WORLD AROUND US IS WAITING TO BE SAMPLED, CROPPED, AND FOCUSED. DON'T SQUANDER A MINUTE. INSPIRATION IS WAITING FOR YOU IF YOU'LL JUST LOOK FOR IT.

LEAVE YOURSELF OPEN TO NEW IDEAS. The only way that designers such as Marian Bantjes can be so über-inspiring is by letting inspiration come into their lives. I get so busy trying to be creative to come up with the next genius idea that, many times, I don't take the time to let my mind connect with all the things that are already crammed into my gray matter.

TAKE FEWER PHOTOS. Staring into the eyes of Stefan Bucher is like staring into creative space. He is an intense creator. Being able to see the world around me as an open source stock idea house is a liberating thought. From anything I see, from any two items I want to juxtapose, I can create inspiring thoughts and ideas.

TAKE MORE PHOTOS. As Greg Hoffman's amazing journey through the Olympics and Nike ID shows, having an unlimited source of photos to look at and draw from to create fortuitous mashups can take your mind to unexpected places. The past is available to everyone. To be able to mine that for new inspiration for future projects is exciting.

MAKE MORE OF YOUR OWN STUFF. Joel Templin and Katie Jain are designers, friends, and business partners. They created a business around their passion for wine. And they've done it without compromise. There are many opportunities to turn your passions into part of your professional life. Explore the options to take that step.

EXPRESS YOUR PASSION MORE OPENLY. If you've ever had the chance to see or speak with Michael Jager you will feel his passion for design. He lives it. Having the courage to try something new and accepting the outcome shows a willingness to keep growing and learning.

ADD HUMOR AND PERSPECTIVE. The wry humor that underlies the creative passion of Christopher Simmons is evident in his work and his person. Being able to keep your work life in perspective will benefit all facets of your life. If you depend only on your creative output at work to fill all your creative needs, you'll be disappointed. Always have a project where you are your own client for perspective and to feed yourself creatively.

DO WORK THAT MAKES YOU WANT TO DANCE. When I look at the work of someone such as Fernanda Cohen, it makes me want to stand up and dance or break out in song. When a designed piece is really good, it triggers an emotional connection with the viewer. This is never coincidence; this comes from careful observation of the human condition and a disciplined hand.

HAVE INTERESTING FRIENDS. I displayed Jorge Alderete's work in the Tether Design Gallery and I couldn't wait to go into work everyday so that I could be surrounded by the workings of his mind. Being inspired by the work of others is very rewarding. Every person we meet has years of experiences encapsulated within his or her body. How can their story become part of ours?

SECTION
02

THE DESIGNER'S JOURNEY:
THE STRUGGLE

That initial spark of inspiration turns out to be a lot of work to make sense of and bring to life. You doubt, explore other inspirations, and then come back to your original moment of creative wonder.

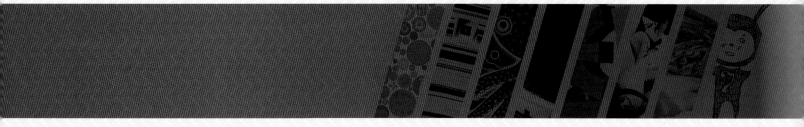

SEAN ADAMS

IS REWRITING THE DEFINITION OF A GRAPHIC DESIGNER.

Sean Adams is founding partner with Noreen Morioka of AdamsMorioka. He has been recognized by every major competition and publication. A solo exhibition on AdamsMorioka was held at the San Francisco Museum of Modern Art. He has been cited as one of the forty most important people shaping design internationally in the ID40. AdamsMorioka's clients include the Academy of Motion Picture Arts and Sciences, Adobe, Gap, Frank Gehry Partners, Nickelodeon, Sundance, Target, USC, and the Walt Disney Company.

WHENEVER WE COMPLAIN THAT THE BIGGEST ISSUE IS THE SIZE OF GARAMOND OR WHY THE CLIENT INSISTS WE USE THEIR CORPORATE BLUE, THE WHOLE PROFESSION BECOMES ABOUT SOMETHING SMALL.

Fifteen years ago, I was so clear in my direction and goal to clean up the world, and finding inspiration was so easy. Maybe it's because I'm older, or busier, or jaded, but finding inspiration is more difficult for me now. Finding a wonderful booklet at a used bookstore, or discovering a graphic novel in a Japanese department store, was endlessly exciting. Today, the process is less about seeing and more about learning. Reading about history, specifically sociological history, is inspiring to me now. How did humans relate to one another in seventeenth-century Virginia, or what political issues informed the Cold War, or how did photography impact the Civil War? These discoveries don't lend themselves to the kind of inspiration that is about seeing, but they move me to reconsider why I do something. But I am a visual person, and I still love finding that odd magazine cover from 1967, or riding through "It's a Small World," or discovering the color palette from *Bye Bye Birdie*.

Like most designers, I endlessly sketch in my notebook, and I have hundreds of historical images in my iPhoto file. All that input seems to get mixed up in my head and comes out when I don't expect it. It's usually a few months after we've completed a project that I'll run across something and say, "That's where the color palette came from." I rarely look at my notebooks, but the process of drawing something burns it into my brain. I would love to say I'm an avid user of design magazines and annuals. But I'm not. I'm happy to read an article, but I don't thumb through them looking for ideas. In the interest of full disclosure, I will admit I spend time looking at our collection of *Graphis* annuals from 1953 to 1970. I'm not looking at them to copy a poster or book cover. I'm more interested in the way designers during that time utilized symbol and metaphor. It's a good prompter to start thinking. For example, I might be working on a piece that needs to talk about "new." I start a list of words that relate: egg, stork, and so on. Then I might come across an image of a gift box for an old ad for Bonwit Teller, so I add gift box to the list. I'm not interested in replicating that Bonwit Teller ad's look and feel, but I'm willing to let the idea of a gift box represent "new."

The concept for the Sundance Film Festival came together when I decided to re-create myths that we all know, but recast them with our own actors, and build new sets using engravings and flat art. I presented the idea, Robert [Redford] was thrilled, and we began brainstorming which myths could work.

Determining which stories would be recognizable became the biggest challenge. We knew we wanted a singular image that illustrated a myth that had components related to filmmaking and the Sundance experience.

I think about the redefinition of design all the time. Whether it's working on the meaning and definition of this for AIGA or dealing with the direction of AdamsMorioka with Noreen [Morioka]. It's clearly a field that is fracturing into many pieces. This is good, because it forces us to be communicators, not merely form-makers. And it's bad, because without guidance, the profession can lose all power and become a million tiny tribes. But I'm more concerned about design's standing with the business world. We want to be respected and have a seat at the big table, and we should. We know that design will be the force that pulls all of the pieces together and makes something a success. But we are our own worst enemy. Whenever we complain that the biggest issue is the size of Garamond or why the client insists we use their corporate blue, the whole profession becomes

about something small. We need to be immaculate and skilled at our craft, and we also need to think big.

We've worked with the Sundance brand for almost a decade. There are basic issues that drive all of the communication. The festival is one component that is highly visible. The process begins with us sitting down with Robert Redford and discussing his thoughts. We ask him if there are any big ideas he wants to explore, or any issues he feels are pertinent. For the 2006 festival, he talked about storytelling being the basis of all filmmaking. We took that conversation and started sketching.

At the time, I was reading a book by Graham Hancock, *Heaven's Mirror*, which, among other things, talked about the power and longevity of myths. During our first meeting, I found myself sketching little thumbnails of different myths. I didn't take them seriously, because I thought, "Nobody really wants to hear about the Trojan War after high school."

We tried many ideas that were all pretty awful. This was the fifth Sundance Film Festival we would be doing, and there are only so many ways to say film and Park City. At one point, I thought about hiring a design firm, and then I thought, "Wait, I have one of those."

After presenting several variations and feeling stuck, Robert said, "Don't worry about me, or what I think. What would you do if I weren't involved and you didn't have to worry about what I wanted, or the marketing team, or anyone else?" I immediately thought about my little sketches of myths. Fortuitously, I was looking through Saul Bass's title work for my class at Art Center College of Design and I came across his work for Around the World in 80 Days. There was something wonderful about this sequence that used illustration and engravings. In the end, this experience reminded me to trust my own instincts and not pre-edit my ideas.

We wondered whether the myth of Icarus flying too close to the Sun would be known to a twenty-first-century audience. In the end, we used several stories: Moby Dick and the idea of obsession; Adam and Eve, which is about temptation and knowledge; the Trojan Horse, for deception; and Icarus, which is about ambition and failure.

Another great client of ours is Larry Nicola, one of the foremost chefs and restaurateurs in the United States. We had worked with Larry for more than fifteen years on several of his restaurants. When he asked us to work on his next restaurant, Mexico, I expected it to follow the idea of Larry's other restaurants that have needed a high-end and high-quality attitude. In our first meeting, he said he wanted Mexico to feel like a vacation, and be fun and energetic.

The key word that Larry used was low tech. This was the starting point. As designers, we are committed to perfection. The printing must be the highest quality, the typography must be flawless, and the forms should be precise. Now, typically, the inspiration point for this project should have been a visit to Tijuana, but this wasn't the case. I was cleaning out a drawer at my grandparents' house and found the operations manual for their Whirlpool dryer, circa 1970. The headline type was a remarkably ugly version of Modern No. 20 with added swashes. "Could we make the ugliest typeface ever?" I asked.

Early versions were abandoned for being too precise. Each step was augmented by the low-cost solutions of our designers.

Years ago, we worked with David Hockney on several books. Spending time in David's studio taught me to work in broad strokes, fearlessly. The Mexico project reminded me of that. The joy and delight we have felt working on it comes through on each piece.

Hola!

ABCDEFGHIJKLMNOPQR
STUVWXYZ
abcdefghijk lmnopqrstuvwxyz
1234567890

When I returned to the office after finding the Whirlpool manual, we started drawing Hobo Italic Swash. This seemed like the perfect font for Mexico. We determined then to use only low-tech materials. The forms and icons are all hand painted, the typography is Courier, the hand-drawn type is Hobo Italic Swash, and the production techniques are the least expensive possible.

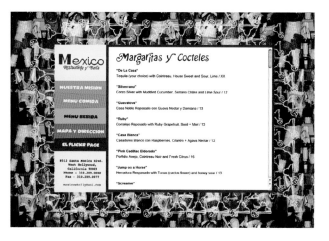

Menus are typically costly and custom. Our creative director, Monica Schlaug, found an off-the-shelf vinyl menu and convinced the manufacturer to make it with turquoise vinyl, which he hadn't used in decades.

When designing the website, Monica came across a homemade website using a repeat tiled image, so we applied this to Mexico's site.

Whenever we have abandoned any part of the project, it's been because the form or design was too well considered. In each instance, we've repainted the image or messed up the composition further. Strangely, it's hard to untrain yourself from making good composition and subtle color distinctions.

AGNETE OERNSHOLT

IS INSPIRED BY DOGS AND CHOCOLATE.

Agnete (Nete) Oernsholt is an award-winning graphic designer and art director with OERNSHOLT, a design company founded in Copenhagen, which also operates in Los Angeles. Oernsholt was schooled in the renowned Scandinavian design tradition and is influenced by her wide experience within the fashion industry. Nete is a former art director at Bergsoe, Denmark, and was a brand design manager with the LEGO Group.

IT WOULD BE GREAT TO HAVE AN EXCUSE TO TAKE OFF AND GO SOMEWHERE EXOTIC TO GET INSPIRED, BUT IT IS THE LITTLE THINGS ALL AROUND ME THAT PROVIDE THE SOLUTIONS I AM LOOKING FOR.

I have drawers full of "good" ideas that I never produced. Most I've never shown to a single person. The reason is that for me, the process of getting to the idea is what I enjoy. I am fulfilled when I believe I have a great idea. Also, executing and spending the time selling my ideas often feels like a drag. I get caught up in little details and can make changes seemingly forever. Thank God our business is driven by deadlines; that's how I survive.

Inspiration is hard to define. It is there some days, but sometimes, when you need it the most, it can be hard to find.

The key is to capture good ideas when they occur. I travel frequently, always carrying my Moleskine and a digital camera with me. I have learned that even when I think an idea is so original that I will remember it forever it is often gone the following day.

I get lots of ideas when I receive the brief from a client. Even more come from conversations, even those seemingly far removed from the world of design. There is no doubt that my best ideas come from being social. But when a deadline approaches, I am often sitting alone in my office. There is no time to get out of the house and no one to chat with beyond my three-year-old daughter. At times like these, I need to find inspiration in the things around me.

Maybe I should get a dog. That way, I could be outside running with my dog instead of sitting here. But my deadline is approaching, and I end up designing packaging looking like my kitchen table, with four legs.

Yes, this is chocolate packaging that looks like a table. I think maybe this idea was a bit too avant-garde for my client, since they went with a more traditional idea of mine. But I still love it, mainly because it is original, and I have never seen anything like it.

XOCOATL

OH, SO' DARK

Dark Chocolate
75% Cocoa

Summerbird

Denmark

XOCOATL

SO' MILK

Milk Chocolate with Caramelized
Provence Orange and Almonds

Summerbird

Denmark

XOCOATL

SO' DARK

Dark Chocolate 67% Cocoa with
Provence Orange and A

Summerbi

Denmark

XOCOATL

SO' WHITE

White Chocolate with Caramelized
Almonds and Spices

Summerbird

Denmark

I have stacks of books and magazines around me, things I buy at the bookstore next to the playground when I'm chilling with the stroller and a coffee. I like to browse through them to see how other art directors and designers work. Sometimes, it is inspiring; other times, I get upset if I see a great and simple idea: Why didn't I come up with that? I sit in my office, thinking, and I tell myself I need to go for a run or do something physical, but, instead, I just look out the window and watch other people running up and down the canyon with their dogs.

My experience with projects such as these tells me that I'm surrounded by inspiration everywhere, everyday. It would be great to have an excuse to take off and go somewhere exotic to get inspired, but it is the little things all around me that provide the solutions I am looking for.

Why does chocolate always have to be wrapped in warm, earthy, velvety, yummy colors? What would happen if I used cold, harsh black and white for chocolate packaging? That way, I would cut out production costs, and surely that would make my Danish client happy. (Or am I just lazy?)

These four chocolate bars wrapped in bar codes are some of my client's best-selling products. They have been around for several years now, and the four different flavors named So White, So Milk, So Dark, and Oh, So Dark are very popular among chocolate fans.

Truth be told, I need chocolate to get inspired; after all, I am a woman. I am very lucky that one of my long-term clients, Summerbird, is a gourmet chocolate maker, and when working on their packaging projects, I automatically receive the contents for the mock-ups. After consuming several packages of chocolate, I need a break, and I certainly need to brush my teeth, and from there comes my next inspiration.

This product, called Rembrandt's Chocolate Spread, is one of my client's most popular products. It has been around for several years and has been featured in design books and magazines such as Wallpaper.

11

JOEL NAKAMURA

TRAVELS THE WORLD JUST TO STAY INSPIRED.

Born in Los Angeles sometime between the Korean War and the Bay of Pigs, Joel Nakamura is a graduate of the world-renowned Art Center College of Design in Pasadena, California, where he later became an instructor. He currently resides and works in Santa Fe, New Mexico, where his surroundings can clearly be identified in his vast body of work. His work has been featured in newspapers and magazines around the world, and he has had many one-man shows. Today, he counts two young persons—his children—as the sources for some of his most compelling and intriguing ideas in paint. "They are my greatest work of art, my greatest inspiration in life," he says.

WHEN I FIND I'M PRETTY GOOD AT SOMETHING, I GIVE IT UP TO START SOMETHING NEW.

Every now and then, when I find I'm pretty good at something, I give it up to start something new. I do it to expand who I am, and I find it's good for creativity. It takes me out of my comfort zone and back to a beginner's mind, which is hard to get back to when you've been doing this as long as I have.

For example, I quit playing softball after twenty years and starting taking aikido. I was horrible at first because it takes awhile to get the proper mindset and learn your way around something new. The new paintings I'm doing are about things that go on in aikido and the martial arts influence. It's about bringing in Japanese pop influence and things that are going on in the art scene.

Inspiration is everything for me. Everyone I meet and everything I see inspires me. I go to a lot of museums to recharge my batteries and to see things from the past— sculpture, paintings, art objects, or architecture. I make doodles in a notebook, buy a postcard, or sneak a photo. I also have a big library of art books and history books I go through when I'm in a dead zone, hoping they will trigger something in my brain, give me a direction to explore. Really, everything is influenced by something else. We're a product of what goes on around us visually and culturally. There's a visual language that changes every decade or so, and as visual people, we need to be aware of these changes and adapt to them.

For my Japanese pop series, I made canvases out of metal. I use metal or plastic or wood or whatever is around. The self-generated work that I do gets me work and expands me creatively. It's like a snapshot of what goes on in my mind. People will see that and say they want to do something like that for a client. Constrictions can also be inspiring. When the field is too wide open, it's hard to know where to go and what to do— you feel lost with no direction. Some parameters actually make me more creative.

I'm focusing on Japan and getting in touch with my heritage, assimilating that culture into my artwork.

I'm getting back in touch with my own heritage through aikido. My parents were put in concentration camps, so when I was growing up, they were cautious about me being too Japanese. They wanted me to assimilate into southern California culture and not stand out too much, as I was one of the few Asian people in my city. So, I grew up more American than Japanese. With aikido, I'm getting back in touch with who my ancestors are. All the aikido movements are in the Japanese language. It is touching something inside me more than anything else ever has.

I'm combining Japanese sensibilities with aikido as my inspiration and finding it to be very powerful. Aikido is all defensive, and you use your opponents' energy to put them in an armlock or other defensive move. This blend of energies is creeping into my paintings.

Now that I know how to throw someone with a wrist turn and take the fall from it, I thought it would be fun to create Ultraman characters doing these aikido moves.

This is Ultraman, a Japanese character from the 1970s. He was the sci-fi answer to Star Trek *in the United States, and he's become a cult figure ever since. He's practicing aikido on monsters and other characters from the show.*

I paint Ultraman characters practicing different aikido throws. I use my son's plastic action figures as models for the details. I paint on metal canvases using acrylic and enamel paint and a lot of materials I don't usually use in my normal illustrations.

"Calling out the language of joy, Mother Family looks down and gathers together her children from all ends of the earth. And a mighty rush of music, laughter, and dreams reach up to fill every corner of the sky."

This Nike project took a lot of culture and color from Mexico. The poem that circles the painting in English, Spanish, and Portuguese was a great inspiration and starting point from which to draw the imagery. Also, tying it into Hispanic awareness and using Mexico as a muse was a great way to tie the knowledge of things I love into a commercial project. It is a good example of a dream project for an illustrator to really showcase who you are and what you can do.

Mother Family looks down and gathers together her children from all ends of the earth. And a mighty

12

CONVERSE
NORTH ANDOVER, MA, USA

JOHN HOKE III

IS AN UNDIGITIZED, UNINDUSTRIALIZED CREATIVE THINKER.

John R. Hoke III serves as vice president of Global Footwear at Converse. John leads an international team of designers responsible for conceiving, creating, and commercializing hundreds of footwear styles each year. Previously, he served as vice president of Nike Global Footwear Design and global creative director of Nike Brand Design, where he provided creative direction for Niketown stores in New York and London.

GOOD IDEAS ARE PERSISTENT IDEAS AND THEY POSSESS YOU.

Inspiration is a funny thing. There is no magic city or store or magazine or book or website. It comes down to your ability to comb through a lot of different things and be able to find the nuggets in those things you're looking at or experiencing. And then you have to be able to convert those nuggets into an idea. Inspiration doesn't come in the form of a solution; it comes in the form of an abstraction.

As a creative person, you have to be able to understand enough about the problem you face and be able to convert or translate the abstraction into something else.

No designer walks down the street and finds the perfect idea sitting right there in a window. You might see something in a window, but it will be the abstraction that you have to convert to something else.

....

My parents had mailed us some Asian pears, which bruise easily, so they come in polystyrene nets.

I always carry a sketchbook the size of a dollar bill, along with a Fisher space pen. I carry them wherever I go, including jogging or just walking around. These are the times when my mind is free to flow, and if I see something, I'll stop and jot it down. I also take pictures with a digital camera or with my iPhone. It's a form of visual cataloging, and because I'm a visual person, those events are retriggered when I go back to those abstractions that I've captured.

When I'm on a run, it's a great time because I have a free flow of thought. I think I do my best work when I'm a bit solitary and doing something that occupies a portion of my mind that unblocks another part of my mind. I probably have hundreds of thousands of images that I've collected over the years and 100-plus sketchbooks, many of which are filled with words or tear sheets. They're a well of inspiration that is a resource for me. I have some ideas that I've never used and some I use over and over. The better abstractions or inspirations nag at you. You can't put them away. They are there always. Good ideas are persistent ideas and they possess you. When I feel that sense of being possessed, there's a level of energy that has to come out.

A number of years ago, I was starting to work on blue sky projects for training shoes at Nike. It was around Thanksgiving, and I was home with my family. We received a gift of Asian pears from my parents. The pears were in these unusual polystyrene nets. My son got hold of the nets and starting playing with them, and it got me thinking about the dynamics of this flexible material, and this became the influence for the design of the Air Rejuven8 shoe.

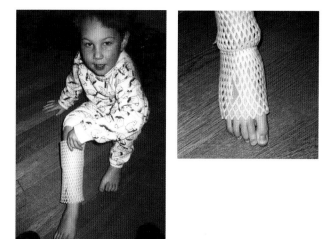

My son kept putting these pear nets on his hands and elbows, and, eventually, his feet. So, here the abstraction presented itself. My son readapted the structural material that is designed to protect this fruit as he put it on his feet and ankles. This showed me that this material flexed with his biomechanics. I told him to stop as I took pictures of the pear nets on his feet.

I brought all of the pear nets to work and we glued them together and started working on this 360-degree netting system.

1·8656

FALCON FLEX

The upper is a fluid, dynamic system that maps onto the foot and responds accordingly because of the exoskeletal cage that wraps around a pliable upper. It actually gives biofeedback to the foot.

My design team and I found that right balance of geometry and chemistry. It was a very flexible, intuitive system that bends and flexes with the anatomy. This project took years to finally come to life.

We released the Air Rejuven8 with big fanfare at the Beijing Olympics, and it has started Nike on a path of looking at the uppers in a new way. This all came from an innocent child taking an object and reappropriating it. I was able to see that, and how it could be extended into a lot of different things. You have to be willing to look beyond the surface and be able to translate what you see. This is an example of one of those persistent, good ideas that just wouldn't go away.

The job of the designer is to help predict the future. Designers are part of commerce; we have to be able to show where the business opportunities are and where the point of difference is. What unmet consumer demand is this meeting? We need to move beyond the drafting room and into the boardroom. Can we speak the language of design and business? There is power in understanding business and where it needs to go. Designs are enterprises, not just art projects. We need to think about ideas that are defendable, sustainable, scalable, and profitable.

Creativity is a nonalgorithm, emotionally driven connection to the human culture. You can't create a map for it, because it's purely the act of being human. When everything else is digitized or industrialized, creative thought will always be that intangible, uncommoditizable opportunity.

LORENZO SHAKESPEAR

TRUSTS HIS GUT LIKE HELL.

Lorenzo Shakespear, along with his brother and sister, run Shakespear Design, a family-owned design consultancy founded by their father, Ronald Shakespear, more than forty-five years ago. Shakespear Design is constantly transforming and evolving by designing in areas such as corporate identity and architecture, wayfinding systems, Web design, urban furniture design, packaging, publication design, and communications strategy.

A MODERN DESIGNER HAS TO DESIGN HIMSELF EVERYDAY.

Sometimes, there's something contradictory about new ideas. Many will celebrate the new; others will find comfort in the known. This is how it goes many times in the design process. Sometimes, the new is threatening. For the client, this might mean my design does not look like him. Or that he just can't sell the idea to whoever is above him. Any designer who has been through this frustrating experience can relate to this. Some will never surrender and will fight until they are kicked out. Some will surrender too quickly. Some surrender too late and will damage the relationship with the client and create a reputation of being difficult.

My will to be inspired comes from the call of a client. I guess I would make a lousy artist. When it comes to the act of design, in any of its forms, I don't have a particular plan. My intuition, knowledge, sensibilities, abilities, and experience play a crucial role in the beginning. I trust my gut like hell, and I am usually right about my first impressions. Then comes the process, which is more or less like everybody else's. My perspectives evolve and change all the time as a result of my growth, travel, music, people I meet, and above all, my desire to understand. Somehow all of that is stored in a blender in my mind and it surfaces in the form of a design solution when I need it.

Design + Conservation + Recreation

We began our work with the Temaikèn Foundation when the site for the zoo was a 99-acre (40-hectare) plot of land in the outskirts of Buenos Aires. The process took two years. The principal aim of the Temaikèn Foundation is to honor our privileged place in this world and to generate a new conscience of the importance of conservation and care of nature.

Tem (earth) and aikèn (life) are two Tehuelche (an indigenous race that lived in Patagonia) words that clearly explain the intentions of this theme park. Diseño Shakespear developed the visual identity and the wayfinding system.

The embryo of the Temaikèn project is the logotype, conceived in a flexible and organic typography and expressing the phonetic name in colors within the range of sepias linking it with earth and nature. These colors are systematically present in all forms of communication.

In all wayfinding systems, there are two fundamental conditions to be carried out. First, the signs must be easy to find and their locations predictable. They must appear as if by magic when the decision of a route or destination has to be taken, and then blend into and become part of the surroundings again. Second, the signs must be easy to understand in a clear, iconic, and verbal system. The choice of a pictographic system responds to the clear premise of providing users with a nonverbal shortcut. While keeping in mind that a large percentage of the zoo's audience is children, the designers created a group of simple and easily recognizable pictograms that represents the different species of fauna.

The various signs on the grounds solve basic navigational issues and provide additional information about the zoo, and they function as part of a brand style, a tone of voice, and a dialogue with the audience.

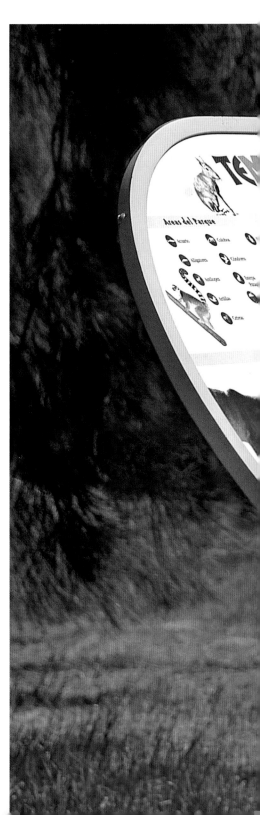

Whatever I have experienced or learned resides somewhere in my brain and jumps out by some mysterious process of activation. I am a designer of responses and solutions, and my creative process is nonlinear. I connect things and ideas and view a map of the problem that only I understand. I keep chewing it, bouncing it, defying it, and, finally, I see something practical and spit it out. Only then do I put it in order so that others can understand it. That takes some time.

My search is personal and chaotic. I focus on trying to understand how daily things work. To design the wayfinding system for a subway network without understanding how the local porteño travels and experiences it daily is like designing a book without knowing how the Western reading process goes.

The master map of Temaikèn gives a bird's-eye view of the park and includes architectural inserts in 3-D. The semiotic structure of the sign system for Temaikèn is formed by six subsystems: empathic, graphic, typographic, chromatic, technological, and locative. The constructive technology of the entire system is extremely simple and integrates easily with the architecture of the park.

Large-scale public works, such as the Buenos Aires subway system, involve complex design decisions because they are intended to communicate to a wide audience and provide useful navigational instructions.

An important part of my thinking and understanding comes from living in Argentina and experiencing the impossible list of obstacles and events that the so-called First World will never understand. The ability to make things happen regardless of the impeding machine is embedded at a genetic level in this part of the world. Each work assignment adds a coat of wit and new variables. These become tools for survival in the business of design. Argentina is a melting pot of ideas. You can spit on the floor and an idea will immediately grow from that. The great difficulties have been the socio-economic swings and the crises that we have been through. However, the country has been very generous to us and it has offered us enormous opportunities for professional development.

Although I have formal training as a graphic designer, I cross over to other areas such as architecture, product, legal, and marketing. A modern designer has to design himself everyday. I don't see myself as a graphic designer. I refer to myself as a designer and my job is to detect an existing situation and turn it into a preferred one.

Our firm does a lot of identity design that is meant to last. With identity and wayfinding design, permanence, differentiation, and cohesiveness are key. Ideas, innovation, and creativity are a way of life to me and are instrumental to those three key elements.

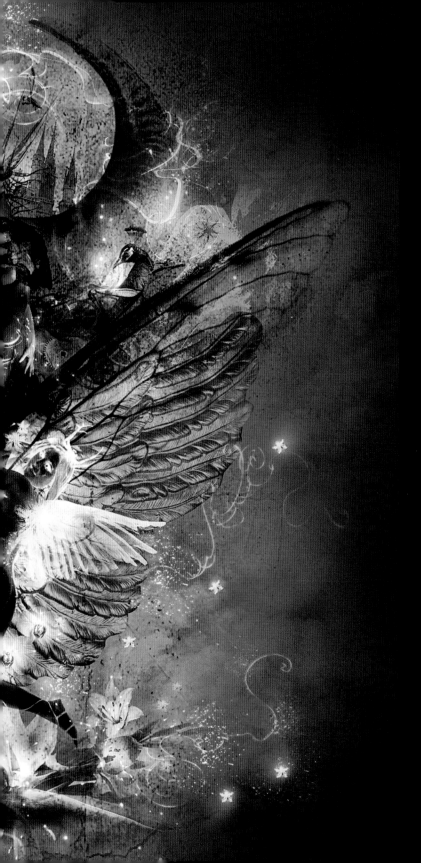

14

ULYANA KALASHNIKOVA

DRAWS FROM HER SUBCONSCIOUS.

Ulyana Kalashnikova is a Ukrainian freelance designer whose illustration styles cross genres and reflect her passion for visual storytelling.

AND, OF COURSE, ALONG THE WAY I TRY A LOT OF THINGS THAT DON'T WORK.

I began to be interested in art and design because of my sister. She is a cool graphic artist, and in childhood I watched her paint and started dreaming about my own works. When I finished art school, I realized I didn't want to be an artist. I wanted to be a designer.

When I want to do something creative for myself, I always revert to my subconscious. A few themes inspire me: pain, death, time, and erotica. And there is a set of characters and symbols, such as insects, women, and flowers, which I favor. So, I just dive into my mind and see where it takes me.

Along the way, I take photographs to remember details. Sometimes, the ideas return to me or sometimes they exist in the background.

The question of where pure ideas come from is interesting. How can the human brain generate something absolutely new if all of its impressions come from the outside world? For example, a person could see a fish and a woman and then create a mermaid, but a fish and a woman are not the person's own creatures. So, inspiration, influence, and imitation are interdependent processes.

Many times when I'm starting an illustration, I have a cloudy idea in my mind, and then I collect material to begin making it clear. It could be photos or works of art of other artists that I review. Then I begin to work. When the work is going well, time goes by very quickly

and I don't remember my work process. Most of my ideas come from my subconscious, and many of my original impulses come from fear or pain. Not real tragedy, just a little understanding that life is mysterious and pitiless.

And, of course, along the way I try a lot of things that don't work.

....

First, I started with some sketches, not for understanding how I would work, but to understand what I would draw.

From initial idea, to sketch to finished piece, I let my subconscious take me where it needs to go.

15

WANG XU

BELIEVES IN PURE CONCEPTS, NOT PURE INSPIRATION.

Wang Xu is a graduate of the design department of the Guangzhou Fine Arts College. After working for more than ten years as a graphic designer in Hong Kong, Wang founded Wang Xu & Associates Ltd. in Guangzhou, China, in 1995. He is a professor at Hunan University and design director of Guangdong Museum of Art. His work has been featured in publications such as *Print*, *Idea*, *High Quality*, and *Graphis*. His works are part of the collections of the Museum für Kunst und Gewerbe, Brandenburgische Kunstsammlungen Cottbus, Dansk Plakatmuseum, and Die Neue Sammlung.

INSPIRATION IS UNIQUE TO EACH PERSON, JUST AS DNA IS UNIQUE TO EACH INDIVIDUAL.

Pure inspiration does not exist. Pure concepts originate from one's own unique experiences, judgments, and creations. Since inspiration is part of a designer's life, it would be unique to each person, just as DNA or a person's dreams is unique to each individual.

During my career, I don't use my inspiration for a project just once and then discard it. If it's a good inspiration, I'll continue building on it.

welcome
BEIJING2008

bienvenida
BEIJING2008

willkommen
BEIJING2008

bienvenue
BEIJING2008

The design collective Designers Herzblut invited me to create my version of a logo for the Beijing 2008 Olympic Games, but it is not a symbol; it could be called a logotype. My idea was to use different languages for "Welcome" as the image of the games. Because I used the logotype in different languages instead of just one symbol, the type could be changed appropriately.

The theme for this project was "Rethink, Redesign, Reuse, Re-fuse." The inspiration was to rethink/design two items that play a big part in our everyday lives. By combining them into different uses, with different tastes, colors, shapes, and smells, they each take on a new, interesting place and purpose in the space. The challenge was to rediscover the role these items play in our lives—to take the function away from one thing and give it to another.

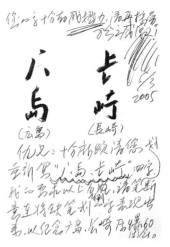

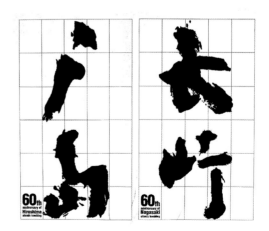

In the posters commemorating the sixtieth anniversary of the Hiroshima and Nagasaki atomic bombings, I used the incomplete Kanji characters of Hiroshima and Nagasaki to express my idea. When the bombs were dropped I felt hopelessness and terror—these beautiful cities were turned to scorched earth in a second. I used the incomplete characters to express my feelings.

THE PEN IS MIGHTIER THAN

Bouch =ART
=FRERES

16

FIODOR SUMKIN

DESIGNS FROM INSTINCT.

Fiodor Sumkin grew up in Russia and now lives and works in Paris and Amsterdam. His fresh style of illustration and his uniquely designed typographic work complement each other beautifully. His clients include *Esquire*, the *New York Times*, *Rolling Stone*, Burton Snowboards, Amnesty International, and Proctor & Gamble.

I NEVER START WORKING BEFORE I CAN ENVISION THE FINAL RESULT.

I have a few Moleskines, but most of the time, they're nowhere to be found, so I end up sketching on random pieces of paper, receipts, stickers—anything I come across. A lot of times, these sketches from the early stages get lost in the process, or sometimes the ideas get transformed into something new. Whatever I am working on, I try to maintain the original concept. Beginning artists and designers often face a problem when they get carried away by the process and let it guide them. As a result, they get total rubbish because they missed something vital in the first stage.

For an artist, the heart is most important. Today, about 90 percent of my work is pure instinct and only 10 percent is based on logic. This is the only way to approach a new project if you don't want to risk someone saying,

"I've seen something like this before." By working this way, you can end up with something that is not imitation, but is uniquely yours.

Working across disciplines is very exciting, and many talented designers and artists can do that, but to be honest, it's a bit strange for me. It's almost like trusting a translation of Japanese poetry to an interpreter working with Russian and English texts.

Nike Reuse-A-Shoe was one of my most interesting projects during the past six months. It's very rare that I get complete freedom like I got with this project. Usually, I can get that only in my personal projects. I think I was probably inspired by a Renaissance painting or a short story by Dostoyevsky. I've been reading lots of Russian classic literature lately.

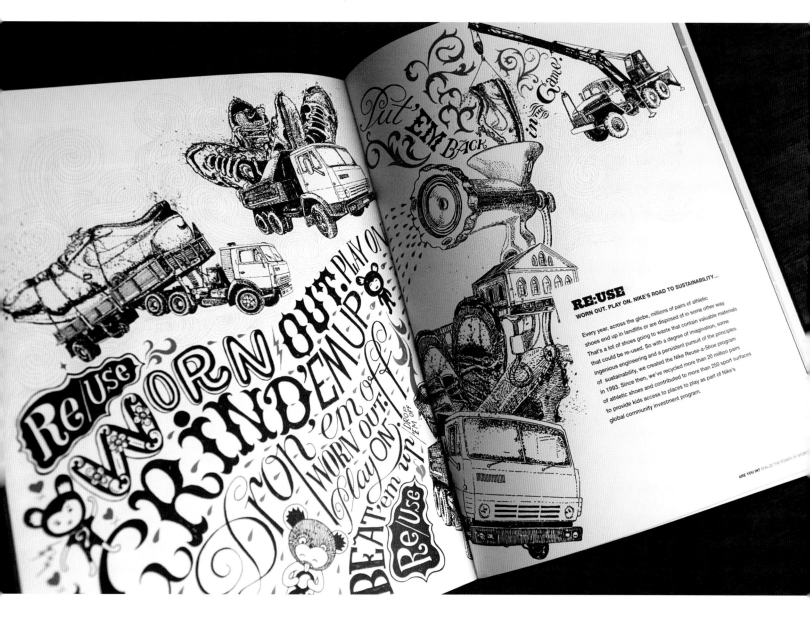

RE:USE
WORN OUT. PLAY ON. NIKE'S ROAD TO SUSTAINABILITY...

Every year, across the globe, millions of pairs of athletic shoes end up in landfills or are disposed of in some other way. That's a lot of shoes going to waste that contain valuable materials that could be re-used. So with a degree of imagination, some ingenious engineering and a persistent pursuit of the principles of sustainability, we created the Nike Reuse-a-Shoe program in 1993. Since then, we've recycled more than 20 million pairs of athletic shoes and contributed to more than 250 sport surfaces to provide kids access to places to play as part of Nike's global community investment program.

Everything comes spontaneously for me. I don't have a nine-to-five job. My profession is my life. So, my brain is in the "on" mode twenty-four hours a day. I never trash anything. In fact, I prefer using the word *decline* or *change*. There can be up to ten or twenty versions if the project is big and if there's sufficient time.

I never start working before I can envision the final result. The "come what may" motto can apply to your personal life, but never to work. There is never an unforeseen situation in graphic design or illustration or in creating a typeface.

Figuratively speaking, there's never a brick falling down onto your head when you've planned something thoroughly. It's better to think for a couple of days and then implement the project in a couple of hours.

I often experiment with new forms. I already have quite an impressive collection. When there's a commercial commission, I test it against my newest ideas to see if it fits.

THE STRUGGLE REDUX

I'VE HAD SUCCESSES AND MADE MISTAKES ON MY DESIGN JOURNEY. BUT I CONTINUALLY LEARN VALUABLE LESSONS FROM THE EXAMPLE AND WISDOM OF OTHERS WHEN I LIVE EACH DAY WITH MY DESIGN EYES WIDE OPEN.

BE YOURSELF. If you've ever laughed with Sean Adams, you know he is without guile. If we are honest about who we are and try not to pretend to be something we're not, our gaps will be quickly opened to ideas and inspirations. We will become smarter, more intuitive, and better able to mine our own experiences and interests for creative solutions.

IT'S RIGHT THERE IN FRONT OF YOU. The more I search for inspiration in exotic places, the more I realize, like Agnete Oernsholt, that a brilliant creative solution is under your hands or in your refrigerator. Great thinkers find ideas from the world around them— even the seemingly mundane can spark creative solutions.

GET OUT OF YOUR COMFORT ZONE. I was creative director at Nike, Lego, and Starbucks. These were incredible companies that I worked for. One of the reasons that I moved on from each of these companies was to get out of my comfort zone. We get good at what we practice day after day. And like Joel Nakamura, when we chart a new course, we will find surprising sources of inspiration that will ultimately enhance who we are and make our futures even more rewarding.

LOOK FOR MAGIC IN THE MUNDANE. Being able to convert the ordinary into something amazing is what great creative minds have always done. Designers like John Hoke are able to look at the world with a child-like perspective. Everything is wonder-worthy and fodder for creative problem solving. And out of that simple curiosity come magical solutions.

THE CLIENT IS THE CLIENT. We are hired to do work for our clients. I've always been bothered when designers speak disparagingly of their clients as though we, as designers, are somehow smarter than they are. Lorenzo Shakespear reminds me that the client is the catalyst for our work. They are the ones who bring the spark of the idea to us, and we have the opportunity to turn it into something touchable, craveable, and sellable.

DESIGN CAN CHANGE. Whether it's the eclectic talents of Ulyana Kalashnikova, Fiodor Sumkin, or Wang Xu, I'm reminded that design can spark wonder and provoke. As designers, we have some of the most powerful tools on Earth. We have the visual acumen to make the unreal look real. We can charge emotions and alter the future. What will we do with the power we have?

SECTION

03

THE DESIGNER'S JOURNEY:
THE WORK

That initial idea turns into a full-fledged project that is a design problem to be solved. All rocks are overturned and all angles are explored to come up with the perfect combination of elements to tell a compelling visual story.

feng

向布者住葆走
文線梦

Beth Zollars PROPRIETOR

5029 W. 119TH, OVERLAND PARK, KS 66209

P 913.498.0530   F 913.498.0565

E BETH@FENGLOOKEAST.COM

17

WILLOUGHBY DESIGN GROUP
KANSAS CITY, MO, USA

ANN WILLOUGHBY

KEEPS HER INSPIRATION TANK FULL WITH LIFE.

Ann is the president and creative director of Willoughby Design Group, a brand innovation and identity design firm she founded in 1978. Willoughby Design Group has developed brand identity systems for numerous groundbreaking retail start-ups as well as creating innovative products, communications, and brand experiences through its holistic approach to design and business. A former board member of the AIGA National Board of Directors, Ann is a founding member of the national board for the AIGA Center for Brand Experience and is an AIGA Fellow.

I DON'T THINK OF DESIGN AS BEING OUTSIDE THE REST OF LIFE. IT'S JUST PART OF LIFE.

I like to keep my inspiration tank full. My sketchbook is a touch point in my life. I tend to use it when I'm traveling because all my senses are open and I'm able to get outside myself and experience the world. Also, I try to find a way to meditate and get out of myself as many times a week as I can—it allows my brain to not concentrate on getting something done. I like my inspiration to come from direct experience. I like to read and travel. I like to experience culture and people. Art, geography, history, politics—all of these things come together to inspire me at any moment.

I don't think of design as being outside the rest of life. It's just part of life.

Whenever we start a new project at my firm, we have a brainstorming session with all the designers. We always try to understand the audience so that we can create a story they will connect with. We come up with a lot of ideas, and everyone will go off on their own and work on it and then we'll meet the next day. It's truly collaborative. Designers are writers and writers are designers. And together we're doing what none of us can do alone. This collaboration allows people to really let go, and we have complete faith that we can get there.

....

I had traveled to China and watched the ancient culture of Beijing transforming. It was mesmerizing—just to experience that many people and the food and culture and traditions.

....

I have a wonderful employee, Stephanie Lee, from Hong Kong. We traveled together to China, where I met her parents, and she really helped us soak it all in and learn.

I've been doing this for so long that we know how to engage our clients and truly do this together so that everyone has fun in the process. We know it's not going to be perfect, but we'll do great work. Our clients are truly involved. I'm sure a lot of our clients will say, "I designed this," and in a sense, they did. The results they see tend to be pleasant surprises and not "How did you come up with *that*?"

In the end, *compromise* isn't a bad word. When you're working with a client, you're serving them. They pay you money. You want to make sure what you deliver is of value.

Recently, after returning from a trip to China, I met a woman who wanted to start a store where she would bring Chinese culture to the middle of Kansas. She had been collecting art and clothing and tea from China. She came to us with a name and a dream.

I wanted to bring as many emotional experiences from Chinese culture as possible into the design. I wanted customers to walk into that store and feel as though they were in another culture. Everything we did was about creating that experience.

We analyzed how people shop and buy in the United States, and we thought about little London boutiques and how you discover and touch and experience with your senses. We made a list of what we thought would work, and then we went about creating that. We wanted there to be surprises.

We created inspiration boards and sat down and talked about the brand attributes. We discussed the kind of imagery and words we wanted to use to create this experience. How could we do this without using the traditional reds and golds? (Photography by Dan White)

影交错
蝴蝶梦

向 东 看
往 前 走

Essence of feng

LOOK EAST

PAST THE HORIZON

REFLECTIONS DANCE AS ONE

BUTTERFLY DREAM

feng 风

FASHION

HOME

ANTIQUES

TEA

Stephanie was able to help us develop the brand language with calligraphy, symbolism, and poetry.

There is a tearoom where they sell special teas that the owner creates throughout the year. We had an opportunity to not only design the tea packaging but also to name the teas.

Traditional Chinese stores do not merchandise the way we do it in the United States, so we needed to combine that essence with an American sensibility.

One of the things I have learned over the years is how to bridge this communication gap with our clients and how to present. You tell stories. You talk about where you've been and where you're going to take them. Great design is about storytelling.

What's so great about this project is that we were able to understand the vision and then create the whole brand, including the website, packaging, and collateral.

feng风

5029 W. 119TH, OVERLAND PARK, KS 66209

feng风

GIFT CERTIFICATE

To: _____

From: _____

Amount: _____

_____   _____
Authorized by   Expiration Date

Essence of feng

LOOK FAST

PAST THE HORIZON

REFLECTIONS DANCE AS ONE

BUTTERFLY DREAM

影交错
蝴蝶梦

向东
往前走

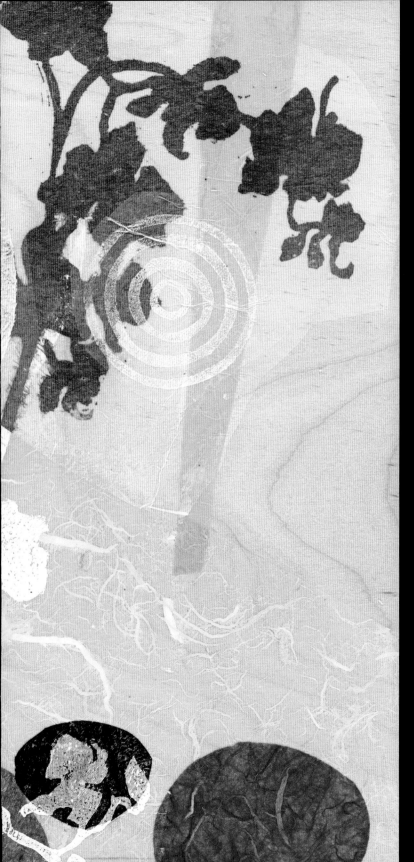

FUMI WATANABE

IS INSPIRED BY HER MESSY DESK.

Fumi Watanabe is a designer, painter, illustrator,
and conceptual thinker who grew up in Japan.
After earning her design degree, she started
working in the in-house design group at Starbucks.
Fumi combines her graphic design training with
her passion for illustration and art in both her
work and her personal projects.

I QUICKLY LEARNED THAT MY DIFFERENCE IS ALSO MY SELLING POINT.

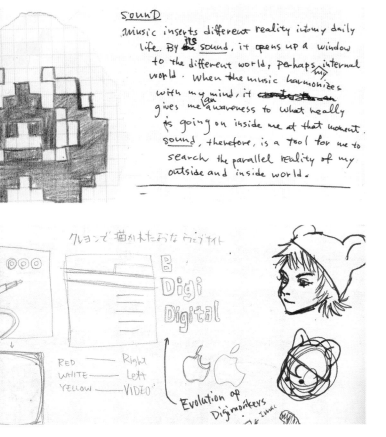

I was a bookworm growing up in Japan, and I was always drawing, but I never thought that drawing was accepted as a career. So, I thought I was going to study literature. When I came to the United States, art was more accepted as an area of study. I went crazy when I found out that this could be a career.

I've always thought that my advantage as a designer was my difference, or maybe it was my disadvantage. It was a bit of a handicap, not knowing the cultural background, including all the TV shows that most people grew up with. But then this became an advantage because everybody's looking to be different and memorable and I found that being a foreigner is really a good thing. I quickly learned that my difference is also my selling point. My background and sensibilities subconsciously come through in my design and in how I contribute to a team. For example, because I work on a lot of team projects I especially get pulled into the brainstorming process where all ideas are accepted. I probably bring a lot to the table for that kind of thinking because of my background.

....

The best way for me to get inspired is to stop, move away from the computer, and start writing in my sketchbook. After a while, the new ideas come to me. I also keep folders of projects—all my processes, sketches, thoughts, references, articles, everything goes in those folders.

I don't want to generalize Japanese culture because I think that in modern Japan, everybody has different experiences, but my background plays into everything I do. I grew up with lots of Japanese books, which influenced me greatly. Also, Japanese is a gifting culture; so many things are gift wrapped in neat little packages. All these things influence the way I think and the designs I create.

I keep a reference folder with all my sketches for various projects. Some of them are so good that I haven't thrown them away. I think one of the reasons I can't use design annuals for inspiration is that it's all in a neat, even package. But if it's in an object form or in a loose file that I can manipulate and move things around, I'll use it.

Travel really inspires me, not because of where I go, but because I can remove myself from the pile of stuff that I build up. It also gives me a chance to look at new things. It's a cleansing process for me. Sometimes, it's not even looking at beautifully designed objects; it could be observing how people do things differently in different places. Maybe it's looking at the repetition of mops and brooms lined up alongside a house or something similarly random.

When I see an extremely well-designed piece, I think it's great, but somebody did it, and it's done. I'm not going to do it or do it better. It's more beneficial for me to find out how it works or the reason behind it.

I feel that if I unload my ideas, new ideas will come. If I share my ideas with others, somebody might take them and do something else with them, or get inspired. Usually, I get refueled from somewhere and maybe even get a better idea.

I get really inspired by how people interact with things. As I work on packaging a lot, I'll put stuff in different piles to see how people interact with it or to see how it would ship. Packaging is a crazy, multilayered thing. You have to start with the way people interact with the package, how they open it, or how they use it daily if it's a multiple-use type of product—how they can keep using it and keep getting pleasure out of opening this

box or tab or whatever it might be. Maybe the break in the seal could symbolize the ritual. There's a lot of emotion associated with how people interact with their stuff.

For example, with a soda can, you pull the tab open. Whether it's a little snap or crack or rip—different things cause different emotional reactions in people. I also think about how something prints or ships, because by the time it gets to people's hands, it can't be mangled. The hand-to-product moment is everything. We can design something that's really cool, but if it can't be manufactured or filled or shipped, or if it's really bad for the environment, I can't be proud of my work.

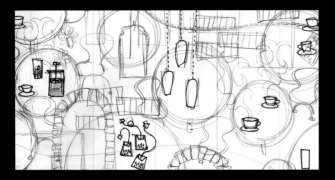

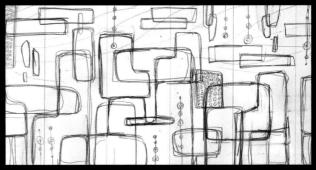

For a mural for the Starbucks cafés, I didn't want to re-create the scene of the coffeehouse because the people looking at it would already be in that setting. So, I initially sketched the café scene and then I abstracted and deconstructed it. Everything was in these big chunks of modern,

bubblelike shapes. At first, you might not know what it was, but then when you knew, you started seeing the shapes. There are tables and chairs, and so on.

Murals are huge and you can hide fun things in them, so I had lots of fun adding the doodles that were in the corner of my notebook. I created them with watercolor and then cut them out and layered them. The act of making it was gestural and abstract, but the concept behind it was the coffeehouse.

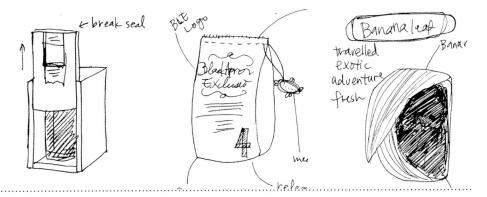

Black Apron produces specialty coffees and they needed a flexible package design that would distinguish their different coffees, which are often distributed in small batches. The challenge was that we couldn't print on the roll stock every time we had a new coffee. And because the coffee was so expensive and packaged in such small quantities it had to be a premium, giftable experience. We explored different structures, from a brown paper bag, which is really mercantile and fresh, compared to tin containers, where the product is sealed and doesn't have the perception of freshness. Again, the challenge was that we couldn't switch the packaging every time, but we wanted to show newness. We sketched and then mocked up several options to show the client.

We ended up using an artist, Lane Twitchell, who does cut-paper art, to create a visual story about the coffee. Then we created a diecut with this art on the box to reveal the interior bag. We found the right balance of the exterior story and the interior look to show something new and exciting. We also created a bellyband featuring the name of the coffee in the package.

Every time a new Black Apron coffee is launched, we would switch the different color interior bag and the bellyband. So, it was just one plate switch, with the bellyband switching out with a dramatic color change so that you could immediately tell there was something new. We also included a little "love note'" inside featuring original art so that there was a little surprise when consumers opened the package.

Coffees that are the best of the exceptional.

In our search for the world's finest coffees, we sometimes come across amazing finds in very limited supply. Offered under the Black Apron Exclusives™ label, these are intriguing coffees meant for those who want to experience truly distinctive and exotic flavors, unavailable anywhere else.

Each Black Apron Exclusives™ offering tells a unique story about its origin, its flavor characteristics and the extraordinary efforts required to bring it to you. They're extremely rare and special coffees, carefully cultivated by dedicated farmers whose pride in sharing them will be matched by your delight in discovering them.

STARBUCKS
BLACK APRON
Exclusives™

KOPI KAMPUNG
SULAWESI, INDONESIA
Whole Bean Coffee/Café en Grains
NET WT 8 OZ/POIDS NET 226 g

STARBUCKS
BLACK APRON
Exclusives™

RWANDA BLUE BOURBON
Whole Bean Coffee/Café en Grains
NET WT 8 OZ/POIDS NET 226g

19

ARTIST
BROOKLYN, NY, USA

LANE TWITCHELL

CREATES BECAUSE IT MAKES HIM HAPPY.

Lane Twitchell works in the tools of folded-and-cut paper and paint. Lane is inspired by his deeply American upbringing and mythologies of the American West. Using a childlike approach to cut paper, Lane brings complex patterns and shapes to life with richly detailed stories.

WITHOUT A LOT OF ROMANTIC GRANDSTANDING ABOUT "BEING GIFTED" OR "HAVING A VISION," YOU REALLY NEED TO DO WHAT YOU DO TO MAKE YOURSELF HAPPY.

The "creative itch" seems a little mysterious. I teach at the School of Visual Arts in New York. Last year, I asked a student why he had chosen a certain color combination, not once, but five or six times. He paused and said, "Because it makes me happy." This, to me, seems as clear an answer to the creative mystery as any I have ever heard. It's a form of self-soothing or therapy. I think I've always known this, and I think any other creative would agree with this student. I think it's important to understand this and accept it about oneself. Without a lot of romantic grandstanding about "being gifted" or "having a vision," you really need to do what you do to make yourself happy.

After more than twenty-five years of being an artist, and ten years of surviving "professionally," I suppose I just use anything I can get to get inspired. Los Angeles artist Edward Ruscha talks about his work being the result of everything he sees; everything he buys; everything he does. It all goes in there, and then you just feel where the pressure builds and then "Kapow," something comes out. And not necessarily what you had planned.

The process of creating an intricate painting starts with an inspiration that turns into a drawing and then one cut turns into a painting that unfolds until you have a piece of art in front of you that will give the viewer the emotion of what you had in your head in the first place.

Starbucks approached me to create some artwork for their new Black Apron Exclusives packaging. They wanted the brightly colored "jewel-like" bag to show through a cut-paper coffee package. I created a series of sketches that showed the process from planting to roasting to brewing. After the artwork was approved, I did the cut-paper art. The art was then digitized and diecut to create these beautiful boxes.

The Dryers
The coffee is spread on the ground and allowed to dry in the sun before being roasted.

The Roaster
This artwork shows coffee beans being lovingly poured into the roaster.

The Taster
This artwork shows the final step of cupping each batch before the coffee is bagged and shipped to the stores.

The coloration of this work is intended to evoke the overheated fecundity of southern California, where the growing season is twelve months per year set in what the Chumash Indians called "The Valley of Smoke." This sky of fiery red hangs over a configuration of overripe green, creating a complementary mashup of smoggy brown. ("Smoghead"; 2006; 72" (28.3 cm) square; cut paper and acrylic polymers on Plexiglas mounted to acrylic on panel; private collection NYC.)

The Peaceable Kingdom *paintings are inspired by the Bronx Zoo. As a metaphor for New York City as a whole, the animals depicted exist in a kind of "tense friendliness." While touching on ideas related to animal anthropomorphism, I hope the expressions on their faces are closer to the nineteenth-century notion of animal nature, than the twentieth-century banality of traditional children's animation. (Peaceable Kingdom [Evening Land]; 2007–2008; 60" [23.6 cm] square; urethane on laser-cut paper mounted to acrylic on Plexiglas over acrylic on panel; private collection, Chicago.)*

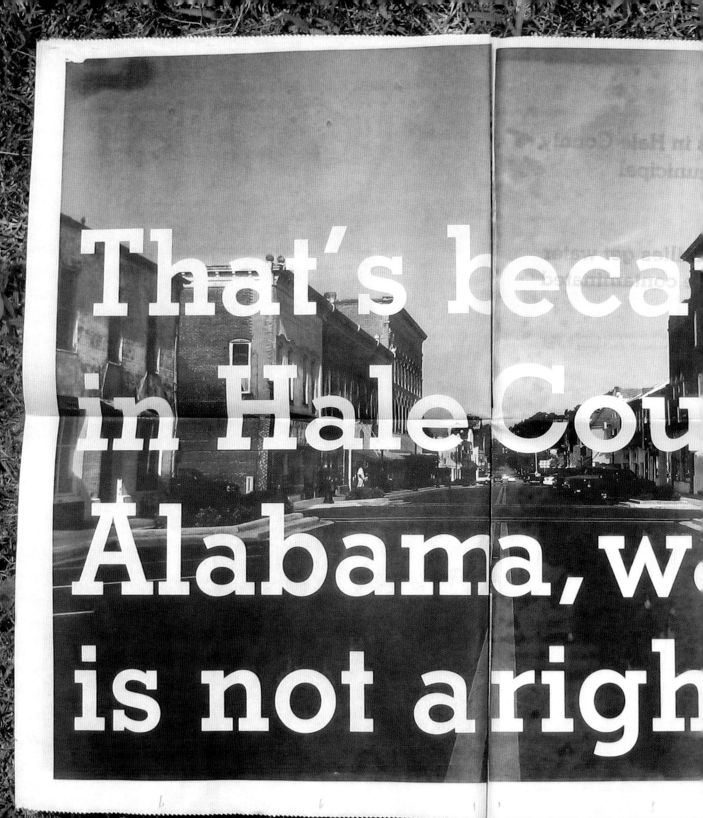

20

JOHN BIELENBERG

IS INSPIRED BY "THINKING WRONG."

What John Bielenberg does best is help companies and their people find the courage and the sense of humor to consider entirely new and wrong ways to bring their stories, ideas, and innovations out into the world. He feels so strongly about the value of thinking wrong that he created a program called Project M that is designed to inspire and educate young designers, writers, photographers, and filmmakers by proving that their work—especially their "wrongest" thinking—can have a positive and significant impact on the world. In his career, John has won more than 250 design awards and is a founding partner of C2 and the Nada Bicycle Collective.

COLLABORATIVE GROUPS OF DIVERSE PEOPLE WILL TRUMP AN INDIVIDUAL MIND IN CONSISTENTLY GENERATING A WIDE RANGE OF BIG IDEAS AND CREATIVE SOLUTIONS TO A PROBLEM.

My own "pure ideas" almost always come from a group process similar to what I use at Project M and MavLab. I believe that, properly managed, collaborative groups of diverse people will trump an individual mind in consistently generating a wide range of big ideas and creative solutions to a problem. We call this process "thinking wrong."

I recently read an article in *The New Yorker* magazine called "The Aha Moment" that tried to explain why new ideas often come when people are doing things such as taking showers or walking on the beach. They discovered that big new ideas often occur when you park a problem to be solved in your brain and then stop actively trying to solve it. When you engage in a "mindless" activity such as running, your brain is actually still processing between hemispheres, making connections that would not happen while you're sitting at a desk concentrating. I find this to be true for me, too.

I rarely write inspirations down in a personal sketchbook, although I often think I should. However, when we run our "think wrong" sessions with groups, we do write ideas down on those big, white, sticky sheets pasted to the wall.

I really don't care where big ideas come from. Aside from legal copyright infringement, who the hell cares? For me, it's all about the ability of the idea to solve the problem in a legendary way. I think the debate about originality is a colossal waste of time.

The term *graphic design* makes me squirm. I'm mostly interested in design as ideas rather than as craft or discipline. There's nothing wrong with craft, but it's kind of like designing tread patterns on tires, rather than driving the car. I'm inspired by big-idea people such as Bucky Fuller and Charles Eames.

In June 2007, I was in rural Alabama with a team of seven young Project M designers. While we were in Hale County, we discovered that 1,000 out of 4,000 households did not have access to fresh water. They either were on shallow, contaminated wells or didn't have any water hookup at all. We decided to do a campaign to buy water meters and get as many people hooked up to the public system as possible. The cost for this was approximately $425 (£259) per house.

Oprah has one.

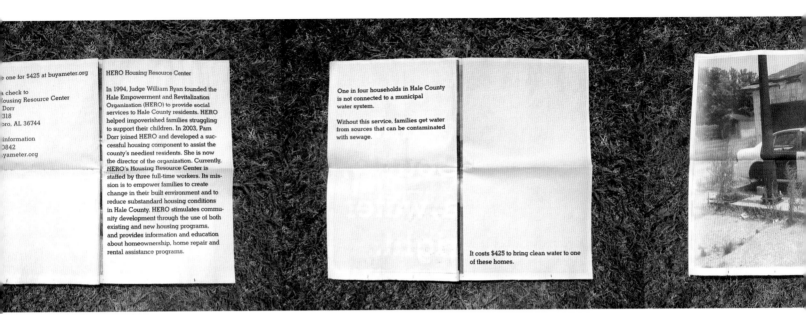

One in four households in Hale County is not connected to a municipal water system.

Without this service, families get water from sources that can be contaminated with sewage.

It costs $425 to bring clean water to one of these homes.

HERO Housing Resource Center

In 1994, Judge William Ryan founded the Hale Empowerment and Revitalization Organization (HERO) to provide social services to Hale County residents. HERO helped impoverished families struggling to support their children. In 2003, Pam Dorr joined HERO and developed a successful housing component to assist the county's neediest residents. She is now the director of the organization. Currently, HERO's Housing Resource Center is staffed by three full-time workers. Its mission is to empower families to create change in their built environment and to reduce substandard housing conditions in Hale County. HERO stimulates community development through the use of both existing and new housing programs, and provides information and education about homeownership, home repair and rental assistance programs.

e one for $425 at buyameter.org

a check to
ousing Resource Center
Dorr
318
oro, AL 36744

information
0842
yameter.org

We had two big ideas. One was that almost everyone in the United States has a water meter and takes it for granted. This resulted in the "Oprah Has One" direct mail newspaper.

The second big idea was to print simple white T-shirts with "425" on the front and sell them for $425 (£259). The 425 T-shirt came directly from insight that Brian Collins stated during his visit to Project M. Wealthy people have a strong and insatiable desire to consume and to pacify their guilt at the same time.

I get inspired by tight deadlines. I remember one late, pressure-filled night when we were putting photos and copy together and thinking that we were really on to something powerful. I think the fact that we were under some severe time constraints helped the process. It was do or die with less than one week to go.

Along the way, we tried lots of things that didn't work. Thinking wrong is about generating as many solutions as humanly possible before selecting and executing the best one. One of the techniques we use is called the random word exercise. Each small team picks two numbers. The first number is the page of a dictionary and the second number determines the word by counting down that number of words from the top of the page. This generates a random word or phrase, such as "pig-nosed slimefish," that they use as the starting point for idea generation. Buy-a-Meter campaign ideas that start with pig-nosed slimefish will be very different and original compared to what you'd get from a conventional brainstorming session. Sometimes, the ideas are ridiculous, but there is almost always something brilliant that we would have never considered without using this process.

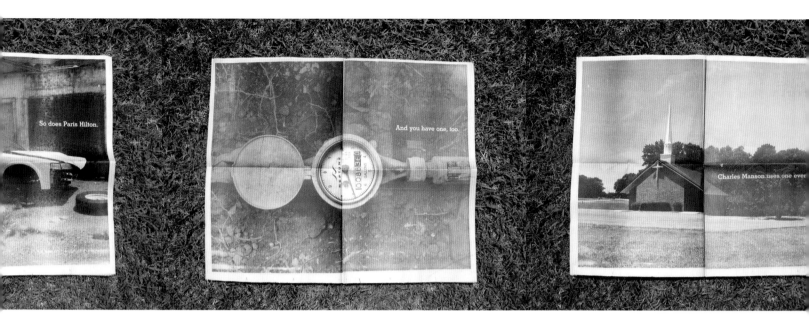

The experience with Project M continues to reinforce the idea that thinking wrong is always useful during the idea-generation phase of a project and that groups of diverse creative people can come up with more good ideas than any individual can. I also believe that once you have a big idea, the execution is usually better with a small core team or individual.

Project M is a program to infuse young creative people with the idea
that they can use design to shape a more positive future.

21

VANDERBYL DESIGN
SAN FRANCISCO, CA, USA

MICHAEL VANDERBYL

GETS INSPIRED BY HAVING PROBLEMS TO PUSH AGAINST.

Michael Vanderbyl founded the multidisciplinary firm Vanderbyl Design in 1973. His studio works across disciplines—graphics, packaging, signage, interiors, showrooms, furniture, textiles, and fashion apparel. You can find his work in the permanent collections of the Cooper-Hewitt Museum (Smithsonian Institution), the Library of Congress, the San Francisco Museum of Modern Art, and the Museum Die Neue Sammlung in Munich.

I NEVER COME IN WITH A SOLUTION BEFORE I KNOW WHAT THE PROBLEM IS.

Being an instructor in a thesis class on graphic design, I'm always trying to instill in my students the idea that you let the problem solve itself. The issue with a designer is that you just have to listen to what the problem's telling you, and it will more than likely explain how it should be solved.

We should try not to come with an answer before we get the problem. I try to listen to the problem, research it, look at the competition, look at the personality of the company, and then try to be inspired by it. I try to find out what is unique about the company and what I can find that is really different from the companies it competes against. We've all heard a designer who says, "I did this thing and I can't wait to use it on my next client." That's something you'll never hear from me.

In the end, designers are problem solvers. That's what we do, and that's what I usually have to teach my students: that you have to figure out what the problem is. You should not come in with a solution before you know what the problem is. The things that inspire me are the things that are helping me solve a particular problem.

I'm always pushing against the problem. I have a lot of respect for people like Stefan Sagmeister, who is an amazing visual generator. But I'm more like an architect. I have to have the size of the lot, the piece of land. I have to have the codes and the restrictions, and then I try to beat the codes and restrictions, to make it better. But as a designer, you can't help but have a style. It's your politics; it's the side of the bed you got up on; it's the way you process your thinking; it's your personal taste.

That's all going to happen anyway, so the more you try not to perpetuate that, the better. I always need to do something that makes me just a little uncomfortable so that I'm thinking, is this right? Is this really cool, or is it not cool? I think that's what makes me keep my edge, whereas if I know I have the answer every time, I think it's time to hang it up. Every so often, if you push an idea to the point where you're asking, "Is this okay?" I think you're growing and you're still learning as a designer.

I got into being a multidisciplinary designer around 1973, really before that word existed. I wanted to be an architect since I was in middle school. When I talked to my high school counselor my junior year, she told me I wasn't smart enough to be an architect. I was also interested in graphic design, so I moved into graphic design, but I always had an interest in three-dimensional work. Then over the years, my company ended up doing signage, street furniture, and exhibits. I kept finding that doing an exhibit had a lot of the same properties as doing an interior, but it had the difficulty of everything having to fit into one 40-foot (12.2 m) van, and it had to be assembled by union guys and feel like a space.

Then one of my clients, a furniture client for whom I was doing all the branding and identity and even some products at that time, said they couldn't afford an architect and they needed a showroom. So, I designed all the components off-site to be bolted into place, and it won an industry award for best showroom that year. It didn't look like an exhibit—it looked like an actual space.

I have a lot of architect friends, and whenever I walk into a space with them they start talking about all the details, the fenestration—those aspects. When I walk into a space with graphic designers or communication designers, they talk about what the space feels like, how it functions, and what it says to them symbolically and emotionally. So, even though I do architectural projects I approach them as a designer, looking at what the space is saying. The products I design are based on that, too. Everything needs to look like it comes from the client it's being designed for.

The first time I started designing products, it was with a small client that I've had for more than twenty years. As I do with a lot of my clients in the furniture business, I served as one of the members of the product review committees they put together. They were excited about three or four designs, and I said, "I don't think these really work for you. No one is going to go to your catalogue to look for that product. It doesn't seem to tie in with what your brand is and who your audience is. It just seems to be out of place." I ended up designing a bunch of products for them. It all just started from there.

I designed a swivel chair that is a lounge chair similar to what you might find in a bar, as opposed to in a conference area, but it still has a business attitude to it. A whole series of simple tables go with it. They're not based on a modern, radical idea, but the idea behind them addressed different needs.

Exit / Sortie

For Teknion, we do showroom design, and all their catalogs, brochures, and advertising exhibits. It's great that they've allowed us to use our knowledge of the furniture industry to find their "place." By that, I mean looking at who they are and what they do and then finding out what makes them different from everybody else, which is the inspiration for me.

I've noticed that at each company I worked for there wasn't really one way to detail the product, because a lot of it is based on how it goes through their assembly line. I realized that if I could just say what the form is, and then have ideas of how it should be engineered, I could probably do pretty well. I still know how to do it and show where the bracing block should be and all that, but I realized that the form is what's more important to them, and especially with the technology we have today, we can really push it a bit more.

It all starts from knowing the company's image and the types of products that should come from the company. That's what the clients expect: how to push their expectations a little bit more and get products that are more interesting.

An example is one of the furniture pieces I'm doing now. A company in Canada prototyped the chair, but because it is a systems company, it upholstered all three sides of the chair and then bolted all the sides together. An upholstery company would have done one giant sewn-together pattern that would have been pulled down over the top of the frame. Seeing all these different applications allows me to question the aesthetic of the chair and the identity it has in relationship to the company and the company's customers.

Teknion is a Canadian furniture company that we've worked with for years. Teknion did research with behavioral scientists, designers, and clients and came up with a proposition called Workplace One. This is a product that solves a need. I designed a product that fits the more casual conferencing idea, where lounge furniture usually was used in just the reception area, but now companies are using it in comfortable seating areas where people can sit around and brainstorm ideas; it breaks down the formality of being around a conference table.

Years ago, I worked for Esprit. They hired me to design their line of socks. I thought it would be great fun. But I found that although the first hour was really fun, after that it was like, get me out of here, because I wasn't really solving any problems. My methodology of working is that I always need the problem to push against, to do what's the most obvious, or do what's not the most obvious.

For Esprit, I designed a two-tone sock that was black in the front and tan in the back so that when you are walking you'll look like you have tan socks on from behind and black socks on from the front. The problem was that there was really no problem to solve, so I created my own problem of "coming and going" sock differentiation.

22

ART CENTER COLLEGE OF DESIGN
PASADENA, CA, USA

NIKOLAUS HAFERMAAS

IS A TRANSDISCIPLINARY, CROSS-CULTURAL, PAN-GLOBAL CREATIVE.

Nik Hafermaas is chairman of the graphic design department and newly appointed acting chief academic officer at Art Center College of Design, where he regularly cohosts transdisciplinary studio-abroad projects that send students to work in places such as Berlin, Copenhagen, and Tokyo. With his company, UeBersee, he designs major environmental installations. He was a former principal and chief creative officer of Triad Berlin, where he and his two partners formed one of Germany's leading design firms special-ized in communication design.

GRAPHIC DESIGN HAS LEFT THE PAGE TO CONQUER OBJECTS, SPACES, MOTION, AND INTERACTION.

I have great visual curiosity; I get inspired when I discover design solutions by nondesigners and when I visit extreme places like the desert and places of rapid change like emerging cities. I also draw inspiration from conversations, articles, movies, conferences, and lectures.

Inspiration also comes from collaboration with people of a complementary creative wavelength, often in discussion and brainstorming sessions with sketching in real time.

I take a lot of photos, but edit them rigorously for visual or conceptual interest. However, I rarely go back to documented inspirations; if ideas are powerful, they tend to linger in my memory for quite a while.

I prefer looking at creative work that is not directly related to my discipline. Transferring inspiration from other areas, such as fine art, science, or engineering, yields more surprising results for me. Graphic design is more than ink on paper. It has left the page to conquer objects, spaces, motion, and interaction. Graphic design has evolved into communication design, transcending and blending all media categories.

The eCloud installation project at the San Jose (California) airport building has confirmed my belief in creative collaboration across various disciplines. If the chemistry is right, conceptual ideas can augment each other in a creative process. Creative challenges of greater complexity benefit from shared input. The idea, concept, and design evolved in an intensive artistic collaboration between me, Dan Goods of JPL/NASA, and Aaron Koblin, an artist who specializes in experimental data visualization.

We used this situational construct, both client-requested and self-generated, as our blueprint to create a visually stimulating and engaging solution.

Starting from the premise of creating a dynamic suspended sculpture that is visualizing abstract data streams, the idea of a cloud evolved organically out of our creative collaboration. Before we arrived at the smart glass pixels, we experimented with three-dimensional arrays of white LEDs, but discarded this idea because it would not produce enough visual impact and would have looked too expected. We also experimented with various spatial configurations and suspension principles before we arrived at the current solution.

Since this project is a public art commission, we had to go through a complex request for qualification (RFQ) process with the City of San Jose art program. Dan, Aaron, and I were selected as an artist collective based on our individual creative backgrounds that combined experience in engineering, data visualization, visual storytelling, public installations, and narrative spaces.

The idea for eCloud is our creative answer to the airport's briefing asking for an installation that would mitigate the visually condense environment of the concourse building and serve as a landmark at the gate to Silicon Valley.

The pixels are arranged to simulate a dispersed cloud suspended from the concourse ceiling structure. The core volume of the piece is 16 feet × 12 feet × 108 feet (4.9 × 3.7 × 33 m) and the pixels are hung from a tensile structure.

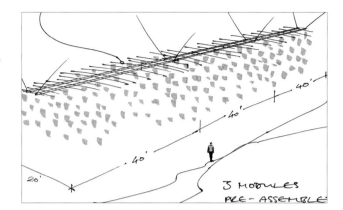

eCloud is a dynamic sculpture inspired by the volume and behavior of an idealized cloud. Clouds are ephemeral and in perpetual transformation; their abstract shapes are constantly teasing the mind of the observer to "see" and interpret. Clouds focus our attention on the sky and connect us with our fascination with flying.

The animations that move through eCloud are based on changes in weather data. The National Oceanic and Atmospheric Administration runs a live feed of weather and wind conditions for all airports in the United States. Unique animations are displayed through the sculpture as guided by the weather at different destination airports.

23

ARTIST
SAN ANTONIO, TX, USA

DARIO ROBLETO

MASHES LIFE INTO ART.

Dario Robleto uses rare and archaic materials, including vinyl records, dinosaur fossils, and impact glass formed by meteorites or nuclear explosions, to tell his artistic stories. Taking his cue from disc jockeys' music samplings, he refers to history, mem-ory, nostalgia, chance, and hope to understand the present. Dario has exhibited in numerous one-person shows including the Contemporary Art Museum Houston; the Whitney Museum of Art; and the Museum of Contemporary Art, San Diego.

YOU CAN HAVE A GENUINELY ORIGINAL, AUTHENTIC THOUGHT, EVEN IF IT'S USING THE SCRAPS AROUND YOU.

I'm a big advocate of cross-disciplinary influences, and the passions I have in other fields outside of typical art lare my main sources of inspiration. For example, I'm a big history buff. I'm also a big rock and mineral collector and I love science. I love music and I take being a fan very seriously. So, all those things play into how I go about making things. I'm constantly crossing over, looking for juxtapositions. I'll make a weird composite of all these influences before I start a project. I don't really sit down and consciously think about it; it just happens. It's such a natural way of making things for me.

I'm really inspired by my passions and interests. I always encourage young artists to use their personal experiences—things they love or are ashamed of. That's exactly where you should be starting as your source of inspiration.

I'm very reluctant to take photos. I have a theory about the importance of individual memory, especially in the context of a hyper media world. I like the idea that everything's riding on your memory. So, when I go on trips, I rarely take a camera with me. I'm not opposed to it. It's just a strategy I've come up with over the years that makes me so in the moment that I have to take a snapshot of everything in my mind.

I do take extensive notes, though. I'm constantly writing things down, like material lists or titles. I've discovered

I will remember something as language, words on paper. Occasionally, I'll make little sketches, but that's pretty rare. I'm such a child of pop music that my mind operates on the song title and lyrics. The length of my writing often is much like the beauty of a song title, where you have to get to the point in one phrase.

I never learned how to play an instrument. I was always worried that I wasn't going to have anything to contribute if I ever got into a band. So, as a kid, I started coming up with song titles or band names rather than the actual music. I still keep an ongoing tally of great band names and song titles. I've given up hoping that I'm going to be in a band at this point, so I use all those names and titles toward my work.

The most structured things that I have in my notebook are the columns of titles that I'm constantly writing. Something will strike me, like a history book or a battle in the Revolutionary War, and I will filter it into a song title. I ask myself, what would be the perfect title for this event if it was going to be a pop song?

I'm also constantly writing new material lists. These could be things that may not even exist. I will just write down the material for the joy of it. For example, I had written down the term *Icelandic lava*. I just really liked those syllables and consonants together. It was the idea of the Earth's hot, boiling material in a very cold place. So, my material lists will grow out of playing with words, and then I will get to the object.

It's kind of a backward approach to object making. I don't know any other sculptor who does it this way, because most sculptors begin with the object, and language is tacked on, if at all, at the end.

Growing up in a postmodern age and being heavily invested in DJ culture, I've spent many years thinking about the authenticity question. The backbone of that culture is sampling. Along the way, it has made me focus on the question of authenticity and originality. Does the definition of those two things have to be that it occurs from zero?

Sampling is reinventing the notion of originality. You can have a genuinely original, authentic thought, even if it uses the scraps around you. There's a beautiful philosophy in knowing a universe exists in the scraps around you, if you just know how to access it or tease out new, hidden meanings. That's liberating for me because it implies that everyone can be original. It implies that the new meaning of the object hinges on the history of the previous object. Sampling, of course, originates in music, but in my world it's applied to materials as well, not just song snippets.

I have a sort of populist attitude in my art. I did a piece reimagining Lucy, known as the forerunner of the human race. It's called "She Can't Dream for Us All." Lucy's been in the back of my mind since I was a kid. I've always been fascinated with her. What really sealed the deal for me when I was a kid was when I heard that the scientist who discovered her happened to be playing "Lucy in the Sky with Diamonds" on the excavation site, and that's how she got her name.

This is a materials list of my piece, "She Can't Dream for Us All": bone dust from every bone in the body cast and carved into the fossilized remnants of Lucy Australopithecus afarensis; bone cores filled with melted vinyl and audio recordings of Sylvia Plath reciting her poems "Daddy" and "Lady Lazarus"; homemade paper (pulp made from mothers', wives', and daughters' letters to soldiers in the field from various wars); ground iron; calcium; water-extendable resin; pigments; lace; silk; walnut; and glass.

One of my passions as a kid was rocks and minerals and fossils merging with pop music in a quirky way. That's why it's always been close to my heart. I wanted to re-imagine Lucy from scratch. If we dug her up today and she was not made of what we thought she was made of, how would that change history and make us reevaluate what we are as humans? I was able to buy some bones from the replicas that have been made of her. And from the exact replica, I remolded each bone and recast it.

Lucy made us wonder about her family and how they might have mourned her. There is an interesting idea that mourning helped propel us forward from the first time we creatively mourned the loss of a loved one. It was that first time someone had the impulse to scream the guttural cry of loss. There is the idea that singing originated in these primitive, guttural cries that would have been induced from losing something.

I love the theory that mourning could have propelled humans to humanness, which leads to the history of singing, which leads to pop music, which is my passion. So, I wanted to reimagine Lucy with all these ideas in mind.

I asked myself, "If I had to pick one thing to define loss and mourning as a sound, what would it be, and what would loss sound like?" After thinking about it for a long time, I remembered the recordings of Sylvia Plath reciting her poems. That is as close to what the sound of loss could be.

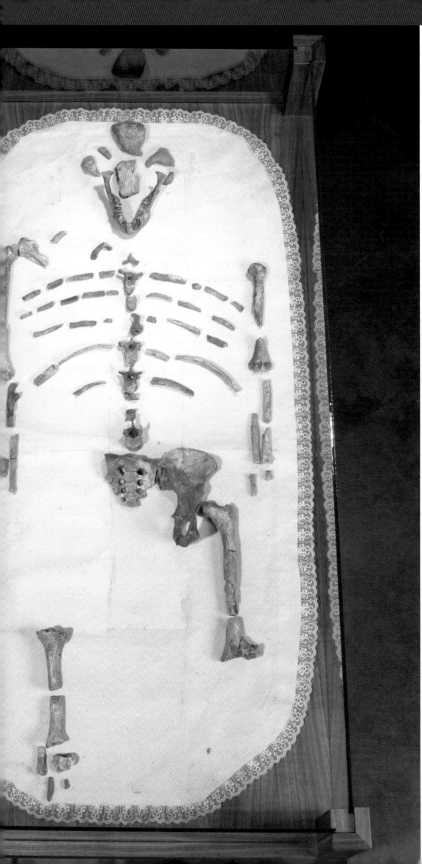

Soon, soon the flesh
The grave cave ate will be
At home on me

And I a smiling woman.
I am only thirty.
And like the cat I have nine times to die.

This is Number Three.
What a trash
To annihilate each decade.

Excerpt, "Lady Lazarus,"
by Sylvia Plath

All of these things happened separately, but came together to influence "She Can't Dream for Us All." I have my memory of pop music as a child. At some point, I asked myself what mourning sounds like. I had the Plath recordings in the back of my mind from years ago. I knew about the theory of mourning cries as the origin of song. I thought of all those things independently, wrote them years apart in my notebooks. And then I just suddenly connected all those dots.

. . . .

For Lucy, when I say the bone cores are filled, I wanted the idea that the sound of mourning was literally at the center of the bone, and that its song was pushing us forward, into humanness, from the inside out, and that we were made out of that. She's laid out in a special case that I made for her, and she's lying on a bed of homemade paper.

RONALD KAPAZ

IS A PROBLEM-CREATING DESIGNER.

Ronald Kapaz founded Oz Design in São Paulo, Brazil, with Giovanni Vanucchi and Andre Poppovic in 1978. As a senior strategist in corporate identity development, Ronald uses words and views to draw lines of thinking, plans of action, identity concepts, and visions of the world.

I PRACTICE PSYCHOGRAPHIC DESIGN, WHERE WE MAKE THE BRAND TALK ABOUT ITSELF.

I feel there are at least two different kinds of inspirational moments. One happens when I'm doing something un-related to what I am currently working on, like shaving in the morning or driving to the office. To paraphrase Nietzsche, you need to be in motion to connect to the flux of life and have great ideas. The other happens when I receive the briefing from the client. I feel the excitement of the challenge, the focus in understanding the nature of the question, and watching every gesture in the client's facial expressions. I feel that this is a powerful moment of concentration and inspiration. I compare it to a jam session, where I try to make the song flow in a beautiful mood so that, at the end, it becomes jazz. I call our method "jazz." Every "song" is the result of this very moment and of the quality of the "musicians."

I have lots of Moleskines, but I also believe in using memory and its power of keeping and refining what is relevant, which will then appear in my consciousness in the right moment. Memory is the first and most important sense, and I try to keep it in shape. The Moleskines are for written ideas and thoughts and for sketching and playing freely with paper—a kind of playground for my hands and my eyes. Besides that, I am a collector, and my house is a museum of objects, shapes, colors, materials, references, and memories. They are there, in front of me, to inspire and excite. Sometimes, I like to go back to them, but not with the purpose of recollecting something for a specific project; it's more like a register of my journey and discoveries.

I think a process of nurturing your skills follows your process of professional maturity. I see young designers running to books and annuals, as I did once. But I moved away from that because of a decreasing interest in the work of others and an increasing interest in what blossoms from my own fight with the white paper. It's the excitement of the free run of the hand and the flux of fresh drawings that surprises me as they appear out of nothing.

As I focus on helping clients build brand identities, I discover that clients love answers and hate questions, and they want us to be "problem-solving" professionals. I like to be a "problem-creating" one first. By this, I mean that, many times, the client comes with a simple question: "How can I grow and sell more stuff?" The client isn't asking the right question. They are asking the same question everyone else does. I try to put them in a questioning mode so that they can start thinking about who they are and what they're doing. In this way, they can move beyond the "sell more" perspective. I try to confuse the client (in a productive way) in the beginning by posing questions about their values instead of focusing on just selling more. That way, we can help the client discover who they are and how they can be relevant and unique. I call it *psychographic design*, where we make the brand talk about itself, where we start with an investigating state of mind, because in the end, design starts in the self-image of the client.

I had the opportunity to donate my liver to my daughter. In meeting with the doctor afterward, I told him the hospital branding wasn't equal to the quality of the service I received as a patient. We scheduled a meeting to talk about the hospital and its values and about how we could express the value of this hospital that had been around for eighty-eight years. When exploring the context of hospitals in Brazil, I realized one curious fact: They are organized in terms of cultural communities and origins. The hospital I stayed at was founded in 1921 by the Syrian-Lebanese Community of Women, so I wanted to explore the idea of a community gathered around an ideal, and a Syrian-Lebanese community in particular. There was also an emotional element at play as the original identity was designed by the daughter of the founder of the hospital in 1921. As we started to explore the identity, I was looking for a symbol that was an expression of this community of ladies, something that reflected the pillar of philanthropy.

My first thinking was with the human element, using dots to express a person and revealing how the man evolved into this diamond symbol. When you focus on philanthropy, your design mind goes to round shapes that express technology and excellence. But the round shapes started evolving into shaped forms that ended in a powerful mandala with a structure of connection, the idea of community that the client was looking for.

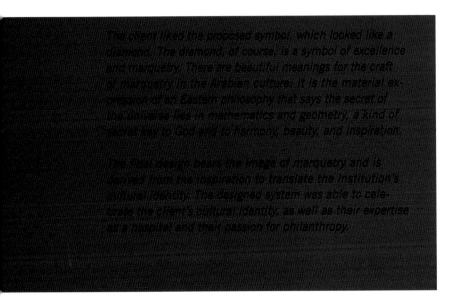

The client liked the proposed symbol, which looked like a diamond. The diamond, of course, is a symbol of excellence and marquetry. There are beautiful meanings for the craft of marquetry in the Arabian culture: It is the material expression of an Eastern philosophy that says the secret of the universe lies in mathematics and geometry, a kind of secret key to God and to harmony, beauty, and inspiration.

The final design bears the image of marquetry and is derived from the inspiration to translate the institution's cultural identity. The designed system was able to celebrate the client's cultural identity, as well as their expertise as a hospital and their passion for philanthropy.

HOSPITAL **SÍRIO·LIBANÊS**

FILANTROPIA **SÍRIO·LIBANÊS**

THE WORK REDUX

YES, DESIGN IS MAGICAL, BUT IT'S ALSO WORK. THOSE THAT APPROACH THEIR DESIGN WORK WITH PASSION, STRONG IDEAS, AND A WILLINGNESS TO SOLVE PROBLEMS ARE THOSE THAT TURN THOSE INITIAL INSPIRATIONS INTO MAGICAL SOLUTIONS.

BE MORE IMMEDIATE. If you ever have the privilege of meeting Ann Willoughby, ask to see her sketchbook. It's like looking at thoughts materializing in front of you. To be that observant and immediate is something to be learned by practicing. We are all walking on the same Earth. Those who see beauty and wonder in sidewalk cracks and manhole covers are the same people who have a stranger speaking about their dog or grandmother within minutes after a first greeting. Fill up your life with interesting moments.

BE APPROACHABLE. When meeting design legends, I'm always struck by their approachability. They always seem willing to engage in conversation even when I know they are busy. I find this true throughout the design world. Designers such as Fumi Watanabe have become who they are through a combination of talent, practice, and plain old curiosity. Designers who ask questions are

designers who are richly rewarded. Designers who listen and give when approached will eventually be blessed many times over.

FIND SOMETHING NO ONE IS DOING. Sometimes, I meet a fellow creative who is doing something I've never seen done in that way before. Lane Twitchell and Dario Robleto are two of those people. Lane's cut-paper art was the inspiration to create memorable packaging at Starbucks. The way Dario tells stories through materials has changed the way I think about the everyday. I find true inspiration through experiencing their art and aspire to their level of storytelling.

FIND WAYS OF DOING GOOD THROUGH DESIGN. Designers such as John Bielenberg stand out because they ask questions. *Why* is a powerful word, and designers are more equipped than most people on this planet to answer that question. Designers are strategists at their core. To solve a design problem we have to assess the landscape and lay out the problem to draw up a solution. What if we all devoted a small part of our time to solving problems that really mattered?

BE A PROBLEM SOLVER. As designers, we are not limited by what we studied in school or what our last job was. We are limited only by our willingness to solve the problem at hand. Michael Vanderbyl helped define multidisciplinary design by being curious and then satisfying that curiosity with designs that solved problems. We can create our own future and redefine our profession by indulging our curiosities.

THERE ARE NO BOUNDARIES. Communication design utilizes every design discipline and is richly fed by

everything from world events to scientific discoveries. The transcendent thinking of Nikolaus Hafermaas reminds me that I can draw from any and all sources for creative fodder. And I can utilize any tool or medium to tell the story I need to tell.

WORDS ARE POWERFUL
We sell the work we do as much with words as we do with the visuals we create. The setup and rationale behind our choices set the stage for our clients to understand our visual choices. Listening to philosopher as designer, Ronald Kapaz describe his thought processes and the passion he has for the craft of design reminds me that we need to constantly modulate our words and images to find the pure melody among all the instruments we are playing.

SECTION

04

THE DESIGNER'S JOURNEY:
THE RESOLUTION

All the pieces come together as it seems like this design project was meant to be all along—from the initial spark of an idea, through the creative struggle, and then a beautiful finish.

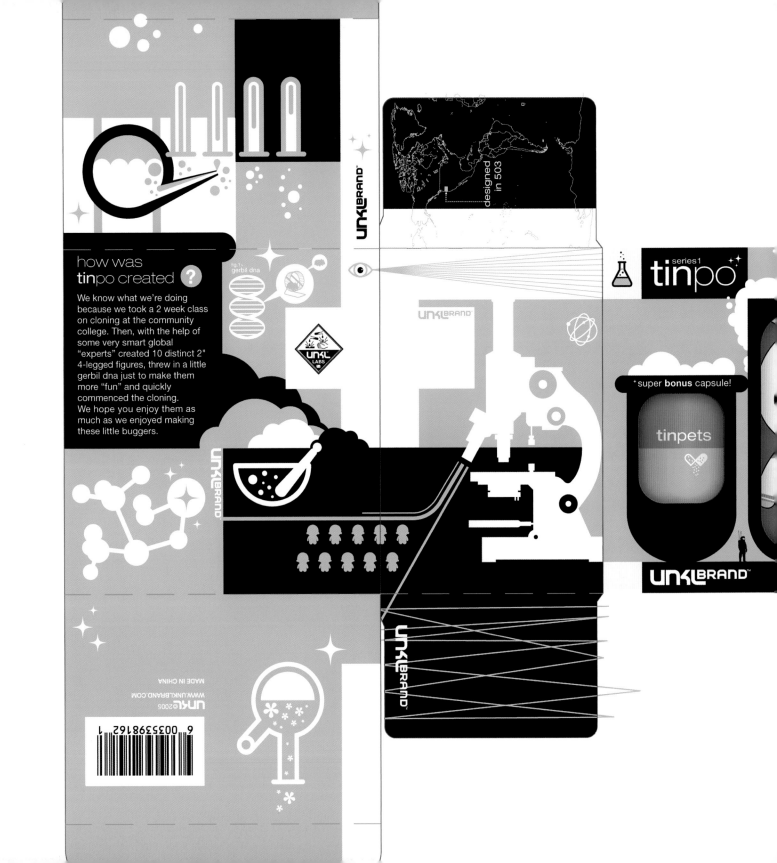

how was tinpo created ?

We know what we're doing because we took a 2 week class on cloning at the community college. Then, with the help of some very smart global "experts" 10 distinct 2" 4-legged figures, threw in a little gerbil dna just to make them more "fun" and quickly commenced the cloning. We hope you enjoy them as much as we enjoyed making these little buggers.

fig.1>
gerbil dna

UNKL LABS

UNKL BRAND

UNKL BRAND

UNKL BRAND

UNKL BRAND

designed in 503

series1
tinpo

*super **bonus** capsule!

tinpets

UNKL BRAND

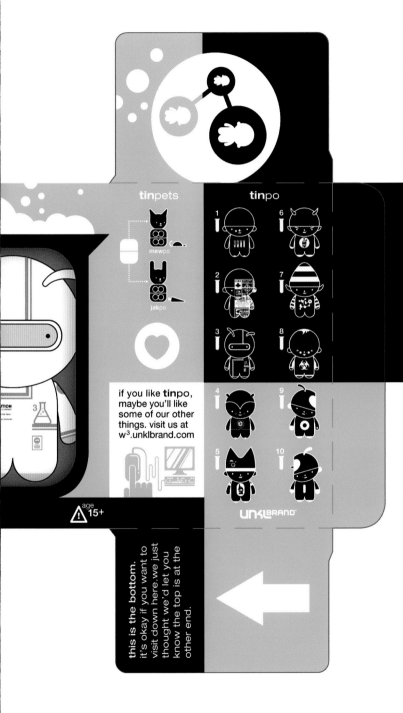

DEREK WELCH

KEEPS TAKING RISKS UNTIL IT HURTS OR WORKS.

Derek Welch and Jason Bacon started UNKL in 2004 as a way to focus their creative energy on non-client based projects. Besides selling vinyl toys, their toys have been animated as characters on network television. They continue to make characters they love.

OFTENTIMES, THE BEST STUFF HAPPENS FOR ME BECAUSE THERE ARE NO REAL RESTRICTIONS OR REAL UNDERSTANDING OF WHAT THE LIMITATIONS ARE.

UNKL came out of a need from within our design firm, Big-Giant, to explore design solutions without real consequences. We were looking for something that wasn't a client situation where we're dealing with the weight of someone else's business. We didn't initially intend for UNKL to be a business as much as a creative outlet for ourselves and our employees, but in the end, each business fed the other creatively. It came around full circle for us, to be able to consider how the brand of UNKL can exist and how the products can exist within that brand.

Opportunities arise for many different projects that are not really based on formal training or experience but on a willingness to give it a shot. Oftentimes, the best stuff happens for me because there are no real restrictions or a real understanding of what the limitations are. You just go for it and let it happen. It's less about thinking what the rules are and what the parameters are and more about just creating.

With UNKL, we originally wanted to design spaces and furniture, but it became too costly and time-consuming to pull off. Then Jason and I started developing stories with characters, and we found that they are much easier to achieve—especially on the manufacturing end. Toys are practically free compared to constructing a building.

Jason and I formed Big-Giant in 1999. While we worked on big and small brands for many industries, we tried to create an environment where the creative process is as important as the work we do.

Jason and I had worked at Nike, but we recognized other opportunities that went beyond the scope of what Nike was doing. We realized we could do our thing with any kind of company across disciplines. We could do things that would challenge us creatively and business-wise. As time went on, we started getting bogged down in the client process, and that's where UNKL came into play.

A lot of UNKL exposure has brought work to Big-Giant. For example, a fan of UNKL called and wanted a robot created for the identity of his company. He wanted something original. That was an opportunity for us to talk about Big-Giant and all the design and branding work we do here. This was great because this guy was already into our personal style and we could leverage that to create his identity. That allowed us a certain amount of creative freedom that we might not typically have.

UNKL is about doing things we have always wanted to do. The only limitations have been time and money. Creatives always have a lot of ideas kicking around in their sketchbooks, but not the money or time to execute them. UNKL is the green light to do whatever we want.

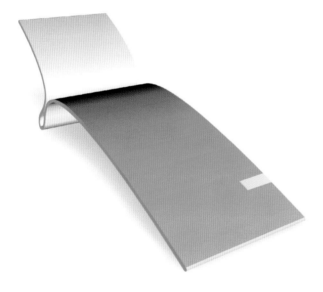

With UNKL, the more we did, the more we realized that there were limitations. For example, we started out designing furniture, buildings, and spaces, but they were too hard to pull off from a cost and time standpoint. It started getting too complicated, and we were losing the focus of being purely creative.

Within the characters, a lot of stuff is specific to Jason's or my point of view that we could inject into the big picture and it all still works. For example, one of the characters is wearing a hat like the Pope would wear, but the iconography on the front of the character is science-related. You could construe this as a commentary on science and religion. It's a platform for us to address issues, concerns, likes, and dislikes. And we treat it in a lighthearted way.

These Tinpo characters came out of sketching and drawing one character over and over again, probably out of habit more than anything else. The big news story at that time was about cloning sheep, and that influenced our story and the concept for these characters. A lot of people were discussing whether cloning was ethical. It was a serious subject matter, so we decided to poke fun at it by creating these characters that draft off one form. Each character has its own personality, but they all look like they're part of the same family. The story is that they were created in a lab and then cloned using gerbil DNA, and that's why they're so small.

HazMaPo was the first toy we released. We wanted something that had an aggressive point of view but was still approachable. It's that juxtaposition of them wearing gas masks and clothes and then being painted in bright yellow or orange or pink that makes our point—the "wolf in sheep's clothing" metaphor.

26

WILLIAM DRENTTEL + JESSICA HELFAND

ARE HOOKED BY SEEMINGLY IMPOSSIBLE DESIGN PROJECTS.

William Drenttel and Jessica Helfand are partners in the design consultancy Winterhouse, and cofounders of the critically acclaimed online newsletter/blog, *Design Observer*. They are recipients of a Rockefeller Foundation grant to organize designers for social change and innovation. William is a senior faculty fellow at the Yale School of Management. Jessica is a senior critic at Yale School of Art and is the design chair of the USPS Citizens Stamp Committee.

WE OCCASIONALLY NEED TO REMIND OURSELVES THAT WE'RE NOT AS EFFECTIVE WHEN WE LET ONE ASPECT GO.

One of the benefits of having the studio attached to our house is that there's really no division between life and work. Naturally, this isn't always a good thing. But where inspiration is concerned, it allows for a kind of organic relationship between thinking and talking and making things. So, if we're at the dinner table and we have an idea, the studio's right there. Jessica keeps a sketchbook in pretty much every room in the house in case she doesn't make it to the studio in time. It kind of works like this: Jessica draws. Bill reads. Jessica starts at 5 AM. Bill ends at 3 AM. Combined, we get a lot of ideas by working a very long workday.

Years ago, a doctor characterized Bill's personality as one of indiscriminate longing. It's actually pretty accurate, and although occasionally maddening, it means that everything is grist for the mill. Books in our library—a library that spills out into every room in the house—are a kind of extended canvas for us, feeding that longing and providing material for the endless list of projects we haven't gotten to yet. So, in a sense, the library is the best kind of memory vault, because it's both reliable as a research source and expandable as our interests— our longings—grow.

....

We started small with our concepts around poetry, just playing with the word poetry—literally, projecting it on the ceiling, sketching it in cotton swabs, and photographing it in votive candles—and it occurred to us that this very playfulness might enable the concept to reveal the many sides of poetry. We called this phase the "poetry is all around us" model.

The line between influence and imitation is a slippery slope, and it's one that we all struggle to comprehend. It's a particularly vexing proposition when you feel you're imitating yourself: Are you being consistent or boring? We argue endlessly about this, and it is possible—even likely—that as difficult as those arguments can be, this is a debate that benefits from having two partners: We like to think we keep each other fresh and honest. That's not easy, particularly as we have very different approaches to work—one of us is focused like a laser beam, and the other one? Well, let's just say that Jessica was recently described as an abstract expressionist. (This was in relation to a template.)

Where our work is concerned, we've found the most significant shift to be brought on by *Design Observer*, which permits discussion, but also recognizes the power of writing as an intrinsic part of both creating

and consuming design. Our recent expansion of *Design Observer* not only reflects our perceptions about this more expansive, integrated, multidisciplinary view of design, but also is a response to our readers' increasingly varied interests. (It's also the fulfillment of what we initially envisioned—that *Design Observer* could cast a wider net on design as a humanist discipline.)

Our work for the Poetry Foundation began as a simple exercise: How do you make poetry accessible, visual, and interesting? How do you reflect its lyrical breadth, its intellectual rigor, its humor and scope?

Phase Two was the Pegasus. We had a copy of Poetry *magazine from 1931 with a Pegasus drawn by Eric Gill. Further research revealed a number of artists—from Rockwell Kent to James Thurber—whose drawings of the winged horse led us to consider ways of incorporating the entire series into the program, which we did.*

And on it went: collateral materials, a website, an online poetry tool, a magazine, a medal cast in bronze. The finished project, as it were, is ongoing.

The poetry project is an example of something that evolved through experimentation and exploration in the studio over a number of years. There was no pre-meditated concept, though when we realized that the word poetry was our raw material, we unleashed a new way of working, in which experiment and evaluation were intrinsic, parallel methods. For something as vast and intangible as the idea of poetry, this was an un-usually gratifying process, and over time we were able to break it down into its component parts.

The most gratifying projects for us are the ones that involve research, writing, drawing, and experimentation. *Poetry* was all of that. We occasionally need to remind ourselves that we're not as effective when we let one aspect go; put another way, the more complex the problem—the more seemingly impossible, intractable, and nonvisual—the more we're hooked.

The magazine, for example, uses illustration, always silhouetted on white, on its cover: The illustrations have no bearing on the content, on the meaning of the featured poems; which enables another kind of form, a visual kind of poetry, now played out over fifty issues.

JULY / AUGUST 2005

POETRY

The Humor Issue

FEATURING

Andrew Hudgins
Richard Wilbur
Michael Lewis

$7.50 USA
$10.00 CAN

27

HYBRID DESIGN/SUPER7
SAN FRANCISCO, CA, USA

DORA DRIMALAS +
BRIAN FLYNN

USE THEIR PRIVATE OBSESSIONS TO FUEL THEIR DESIGNS.

Hybrid Design was formed by the husband and wife design team of Brian Flynn and Dora Drimalas. By blending their complementary yet diverse design styles and methodologies, Hybrid produces one-of-a-kind concepts not usually expected from a traditional graphic design firm. They have also created their own brands, such as Super7 and Hybrid Home. In addition, they publish *Super7* magazine and own the Super7 store in San Francisco where they sell toys, art, books, apparel, and magazines.

THE CLIENT IS COMING TO YOU TO GIVE THEM EVERYTHING THEY'VE GOT IN THE BRIEF, PLUS WHAT YOU CAN BRING TO IT THAT THEY DON'T EVEN KNOW THAT THEY NEED.

DD: I think we'd probably get bored pretty quickly if we were just doing the same thing over and over again.

BF: I think the reason you get hired as a designer is not to execute the brief. Anybody can execute the brief. They want you to give them everything in brief, plus ideas and designs they didn't even know they needed.

DD: We like to work on a variety of stuff, whether it's toys or textiles or an annual report. Inspiration comes from many different places. The more varied the projects, the more varied your inspiration.

Brian and I collect everything, from dishes and furniture and toys, to design books and children's books. We go to flea markets and antique stores, looking for treasures. We'd find a lot of inspiration in those treasures. Our next step was to find a way to turn our collection obsession into real projects.

BF: Our products and our nontraditional graphic design were born out of the fact that we couldn't find what we wanted. For example, we made pillows because Dora spent six months looking for pillows for the house and couldn't find what she wanted. So, she finally got fed up and made her own. It was the same with our T-shirts and *Super 7* magazine.

DD: Brian was always an inspiration for me, coming from a very DIY background. As long as I knew him, he was always publishing magazines, producing records for his friends, and doing artwork for record and fliers. Even if a band he liked was coming to town, he would do a flier to help promote it, even though nobody in the band had asked for it. It's funny because one of those fliers got into an AIGA design annual. Those were two different points on the design continuum, the AIGA annual and a flier for a punk band.

BF: Our magazine, Super7, has really taken off. But that was never our intention, or at least never in the original plan. We started it as a fun magazine about our obsession for collecting Japanese toys. At the time, we hoped that twenty people would care about it. Our point was to just get it out there because no one else was doing it, and it was a way to put that information down in a permanent way and start the communication at least.

BF: We're working on a project with Lucasfilm where we're making a storm trooper, but in the style of the jumbo storm troopers from the 1970s that were made of blow-molded polyethylene and fired missiles from their fists. As a collector, that's a toy I wish I had. We make the stuff we wish we could get but can't find.

BF: Coming from a punk background, no one was ever going to give you anything. If you wanted something, you had to create it. If you wanted a show, you needed to put it on. No one was going to record your band for you. No one was going to put out your record for you. No one was going to do anything for you.

That sort of mentality has crossed over into everything we've done. Whenever we get frustrated, we say, "Why don't we just make our own?" That barrier to entry is always perception. Everybody perceives that they can't do it or they're not supposed to or they're not allowed to.

DD: All of it manages to support itself, whether it's the posters and art shows or pillows and housewares. You always need to do a little creative tinkering on the side that is just for yourself and manages to inspire you, whatever that is.

In your first few years in design you're constantly getting your heart broken because the client makes you change a color. You think, "Oh, this is awful, the client doesn't

understand." And then you realize that this isn't fine art. This is problem solving. It is compromise. You have to remember that there are probably sixty people making a decision.

BF: Now we're designing a jumbo storm trooper toy. In the 1970s, they had 2-foot (61 cm)-tall robots in the states called Shogun Warriors that shot off their fists. Those were imported from Japan, and there were about sixty different characters in all.

DD: It's also kind of neat to take this retro toy and make it into a retro form factor. If you just think of it as a shape, from the early to mid-1970s and the fact that *Star Wars* didn't happen until the late 1970s. They never put these two things together. So, it is a building kind of process, but it is neat to take the things that inspire you and the things that you collect, and then turn it into a new project this way.

BF: Yeah, take them and just retweak them into something that hasn't been done before.

DD: So, there we were, goofing off at the store creating the "dead guys from *Star Wars* wallpaper," which we could do because it's ours, and then we got a small retail project for Hybrid Design. It was for sportswear that was going to go into boutiques. We needed to create a small merchandising presence for high-end women's footwear.

We had this vendor after having gone through the process of making wallpaper for our store.

BF: The wallpaper that we designed for our client's stores looked like a 1970s grandma's wallpaper that was sport and glamour inspired.

DD: If there was such a thing as a sporty, glamorous grandma.

I think some of our inspiration comes from textiles and interior design, and even old children's books. I'm a big fan of Jonathan Adler and all kinds of interior design. So, it was a normal thing for me to create graphics to be put on pillows instead of creating graphics just for T-shirts. It's fabric. It's either cut into this shape or cut into that shape. And if it's a pillow, I can look at

DD: The retail feeds our design work in many ways. For example, when we opened the Super7 store, we created a flocked wallpaper pattern for the back wall of the store. It's a Victorian pattern of all the people who died in the Star Wars movies.

DD: We designed an area for our client's store catering to the woman who shops there. We re-created her vanity area where she would get ready to go out on the town; that was the merchandising display that went into those stores. We designed a new pattern of trophies and courts and shoes and all kinds of cool vintage graphic references that we wove together for the gold on gold wallpaper we created for them. We sourced vanities and had those painted, and then the shoes were merchandised on top of them. It was a natural evolution of what we had done at the store.

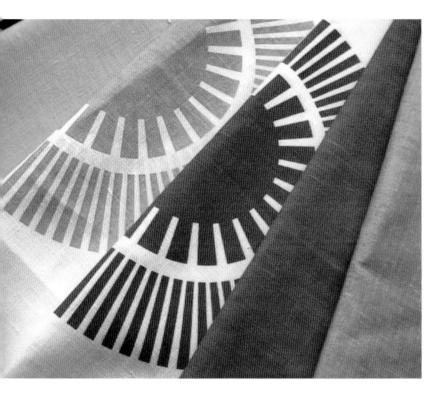

DD: I came up with the design for the Secret Service pillows because I always found something interesting about the "Men in Black"—the secret service, the conspiracy theory stuff, JFK. I loved Jackie O stuff, so all of that is intertwined for me.

it longer. The same thing goes for posters. The medium doesn't matter. Have fun doing the design and then figure out where you want it to go.

BF: With the pillows, once Dora finally made up her mind that it was time to make them, she flew to Los Angeles to a textile show, talked to a bunch of different manufacturers, found one she liked, and then we started sending them tests and they started sending us fabric dips, and we just sort of ran with it.

DD: We started selling them to shops we would go to. It's your world, you're already there. It's just a matter of taking that next step into becoming part of it.

DUFFY + PARTNERS
MINNEAPOLIS, MN, USA

JOE DUFFY

IS A SOCIAL ANTHROPOLOGIST.

Joe Duffy, the chairman of Duffy & Partners, is a much-admired creative director and an expert in branding and design. When he started Duffy & Partners predecessor Duffy Design in 1984, in association with creative advertising agency Fallon Worldwide, he broke new ground for the collaborative integration of branding and design with advertising. Duffy's work includes brand and corporate identity and design development for leading global companies such as BMW, Coca-Cola, McDonald's, Starbucks, and Sony. His understanding of how design affects consumer attitudes has led to many big ideas executed in advertising as well as design.

I THINK THAT AS DESIGNERS, WE NEED TO LIVE OUR LIVES WITH OUR EYES OPEN MUCH WIDER THAN NON-DESIGNERS.

As designers, we need to be social anthropologists studying what's going on in culture. Then we can turn that information into an inspiring message that will attract people to whatever we have to offer.

It's important to develop ideas that pertain directly to the issue at hand. What do you want to convince people to do or be a part of? Who are we trying to attract, what are their interests, and what will attract them to our design message?

Find out what's going on in popular culture, in the streets. Experience life, not relative to design specifically, but more importantly, find out why people are attracted to certain kinds of messages at that point in time. That's all infinitely more valuable than spending your time digging through design annuals.

For example, we're obviously in the depths of a very serious recession, and that is a much more important factor in attracting an audience's attention than what is currently hot in design.

Virtually every project we're working on today is about an experience as opposed to a one-off encounter such as a package, a website, a logo, a brochure, a commercial, or anything else. This reflects the melding of vertical disciplines within graphic design, environmental design, and Web design.

If we're developing an identity for a chain of restaurants, we need to understand what the target audience is interested in, what the competitive set is up to, and most importantly, what differentiates the chain from the competition. We need to establish a brand language as opposed to just a logo or a store design or package. But this brand language needs to be broad enough, multifaceted enough, and compelling enough so that we can apply it in various ways to every point of contact with the target audience.

If the language is based on colors, type, photographs, materials, and architecture, it can be unified by a single-minded notion of what makes the plan special, and it can be diverse enough to apply in all of those ways. If all of those ways relate to why this brand is special and important for the target audience, you have the identity in all its appropriate touch points.

Apple is a good example of this, because whether you come across products from Apple via its packaging or its television commercials, the in-store experience, the point of sale, all the way down to things like the instruction manual, are delivered in a unified way. It's almost like a person. Obviously, they dress differently at different times, speak differently at different times, enjoy themselves in different ways, and express themselves in lots of different ways, but they are one person. And they are multifaceted and complex, and so are most brands.

We all like to think of ourselves as renaissance people, but few of us are graphic designers, filmmakers, advertising creatives, architects, interior designers, and so on. I always love when a client comes to us and says, "We want you to do design, but we want to establish this brand in a holistic way. We'd like you to work with our architects, our advertising agency, and other people to make sure we're covering all the ground to revitalize this brand and send it out to the world new and fresh or to literally create this new brand in a powerful way."

I think as designers we need to live our lives with our eyes open much wider than nondesigners. I always have a digital camera on me, and if I see something interesting in the street, someone wearing something I've never seen before, or a sign, or just a gathering of kids on the street, I shoot it.

After we do the visual brief, it's time to draw. I feel it's essential that designers draw first and get on the computer after we see the sketches. All of our designers have sketchbooks that have thousands of little sketches in them.

The young designer who came up with this idea had cut out a map of the Bahamas and stuck it on a page in his sketchbook, and then he started simplifying that map. It started with sketches and little scraps that the designer came up with.

The logo and concept become functional when you go on the website and click on each island. Information pops up telling you what you can do on that island.

We have a wealth of interesting images in our studio, and we always start a project by pulling from all of those images, some of which we may find on the Internet, some in stock photo books, but most from digital files that we've taken individually.

We take a verbal brief from the client, and we visualize that brief in the form of a collage. In the best instances, our clients do that with us, which I think scares a lot of creative people. But I've found that if we include them in this important first phase of creative development, we get further along more quickly. We create beautifully designed collages, making sure each image is appropriate for what we're being asked to do in answering the brief.

When we build the collage together and use it as a springboard for design ideas, those ideas are going to look like they came directly from our visual brief. And they're not going to be a surprise to the client, because they helped define the visual brief and were part of the creative process. It helps avoid that point that all designers know where the client says, no, I like black better than brown, or I like this typeface or that photograph better, and you've got a collaboration that is very unhealthy and typically leads to bad design.

For our research for the Bahamas identity, we went to the Bahamas and shot pictures of flora, fauna, native dress, the people, and the beautiful environment. We used that inspiration and imagery to build the collages. One of the collages features a point of difference of fourteen

destinations. There's a stylized bird in the collage, some photographs of flowers, some stylized flowers, a hand-scrawled sign from a street vendor in Nassau, pictures of people who had brightly colored clothes on, and some stylized illustrations of the water.

Our concept and the resulting website for the fourteen islands of the Bahamas played to the position that we developed in the design and advertising, which was island hopping. If you want to golf, you can go to this island. If you want to fish, go to that island. If you want to snorkel and be away from the world, you can go to this other island. If you want to gamble and stay at the luxury hotel, you can stay at that island.

Bahamas Air now uses the identity, and people in the Bahamas use it in different ways to express their nation's brand. We established the language and the standard, but now everyone who is expressing anything about the Bahamas uses that language.

If you squint and plop the finished design into the middle of the collage, it should look like it is born of that. The visual collage becomes a filter, and it helps you decide which design elements are appropriate or what the home page should look like. It's not just the look of that collection of images; it's what those images say about the differentiating mood or point of view of this brand.

If you look at the variations that led to the final design, you'll see that there were various phases of development.

It always looks a lot simpler in its finished form than it was in development and refinement, but the germ of the idea was appropriate because it was based on the visual brief that was created with the client.

When the client saw it, it was a slam dunk. The director of tourism said, "Of course, that's what we are." But no one had ever done the obvious before. Now they had something that really made them different.

....

Everything from the advertising to the website to items like beach bags and luggage tags hangs together for this branding execution.

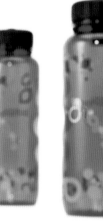

LOUK DE SÉVAUX

DESIGNS WITH POWER AND HUMOR.

Louk de Sévaux is the managing partner of DAY, an international, multidisciplinary creative agency based in Amsterdam, with offices in New York and Dubai. Louk has worked extensively with Nike, Porsche, MTV, O'Neill, the van Gogh Museum, and Orange.

GREAT DESIGN REQUIRES WILLINGNESS TO CROSS BORDERS AND PUT PREJUDICE ASIDE.

I notice unlikely or new combinations—things that cross boundaries. I enjoy learning viewpoints that truly alter the way we look at things. This can happen when I talk with a friend, when I read about a political or economic problem, when I play with my kids, or when I go to a museum. It can happen anywhere and anytime.

Inspiration comes from being curious. It can come from reading a book, looking at a website, or watching a lecture from the TED conference. It always starts with associating ideas to define positioning, strategies, and concepts. Whereas influence is very positive, provided it is entirely unbiased and openminded, it should never become imitation. Other designers' work can play a role in visualizing ideas, not in concepts. This can help to explore the appropriate visual language for the project.

There is a huge potential to rethink the way we live. We can shape our world and resolve challenges if we combine creative thinking with technology and business. This requires willingness to cross borders and put prejudice aside, whether you are a financial specialist or a graphic designer.

As far as designers are concerned, they need to be challenged to think out of their box, whether that box is called graphic design, retail design, or web design. Too often, they show a specific kind of narrow mindedness, an unwillingness to explore worlds other than their own. This is why curiosity is one of our key brand values at DAY: to think beyond boundaries that we believe, in most cases, are imaginary.

Bugaboo asked us to come up with a concept for their trade shows and events and then translate that identity to the retail stores. They required a flexible kit of parts to accommodate different locations, event sizes, and purposes. The contemporary design of Bugaboo Strollers is known for its rugged and functional qualities to the point of effortlessness.

All this talking and brainstorming led to a pile of paper with doodles and drafts. Even to an almost perfect answer to the brief. And suddenly, the idea was born. It was a runaway success. The client immediately embraced the idea. The first event coincided with the launch of the Bugaboo Bee.

We explored all options. We included any possible use of the half-pipe—from a picnic at Times Square to a beach event. -

Bugaboo Strollers set a new standard for innovation, quality, and aesthetics in the world of baby strollers. We wanted to make sure our concepts for these projects reflected their values. The concepts all played with the idea of mobility.

In the work we do for Bugaboo, we look for simple and strong ideas: simple because the product is so detailed; and strong because Bugaboo is a high-quality brand with a strong personality. Any platform we create for this hero product therefore needs to support the product yet be completely in line with the brand's personality.

We start by exploring all options, questioning the status quo, the trusted and well known, to come to new insights.

For this project, we wanted to find a concept that stood out from regular trade show presentations. It needed a strong backdrop—making the product the hero—in line with the brand values, with a clear link to mobility; a concept that would exceed the creative brief, with power, but also with humor. And suddenly, there it was.

At first, we focused on a playground type of landscape, with modular elements. We liked our ideas but missed "the big and bold gesture." So, the moment the half-pipe idea popped up in our minds we trashed everything we had and worked through the weekend changing our proposals.

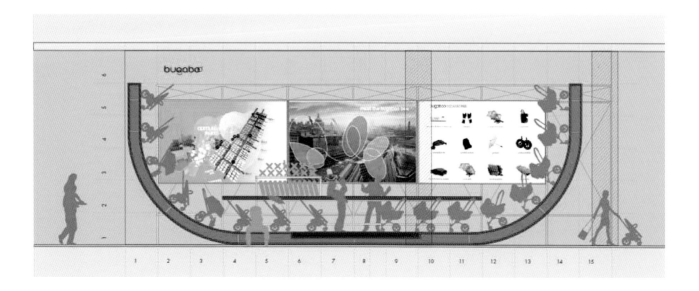

We then took the brief and made sure all functional requirements had been met. We broke the half-pipe down to a kit of parts that can be used on any location, indoor and outdoor, in different sizes and heights so that it can easily be adapted to carry different messages.

We started by defining our strategy for the project. We wanted to come up with a concept that immediately felt like Bugaboo—an iconic shape with a twist; something that would not go unnoticed.

Our presentation covered the whole thinking process. We included all possible options with the concept, and showed the practical side of it in detail. This project confirmed the value of out-of-the-box thinking and of concentration on the clients' interests, both on the company level as well as on a personal level.

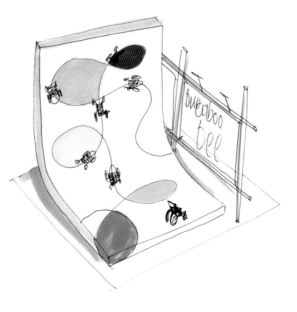

The half-pipe is now traveling the world. It gets regular updates to communicate campaigns and product launches. The latest iteration we developed was to adapt existing half-pipes in urban environments and organize Bugaboo events around them.

30

CRAMA DESIGN ESTRATÉGICO
RIO DE JANEIRO, BRAZIL

RICARDO LEITE

IS A BRAZILIAN RENAISSANCE MAN.

Ricardo Leite is partner and creative director of Crama Design Estratégico, a Brazilian design agency founded in 1991 and based in Rio de Janeiro. As one of the biggest design agencies of Brazil, Crama's team works across all design disciplines. Ricardo teaches design at UniverCidade (University Center at Rio de Janeiro).

OUR JOB IS ABOUT FINDING A VISUALLY INTERESTING WAY TO TELL A STORY.

Creative inspirations come from anywhere and at any time for me. Once, I found what I wanted when I saw the cover of a book about Frank Gehry in the window of a bookstore. It was a close-up photo of Bilbao's Guggenheim, and I saw shadows and lights, black and white, in a very interesting composition. I saw my graphic elements in that photo. I find inspirations for graphic compositions everywhere, but finding the idea inspirations is harder, because I have to look for associations with the subject.

Sometimes, I go to a magazine store and just thumb through lots of magazines. I'm not looking at specific images, but for the ideas that come from something the image triggers for me. It's like a mystical trance. Flipping through magazines is a way to free my mind, a stimulating tool. Sometimes, I go to a dictionary and look for a key word associated with the main idea, and I find relationships with the subject. Usually, I find interesting connections that help stimulate new ideas.

We are surrounded by the same solutions everywhere. People gravitate toward what they already know. It's like a child wanting to listen to the same story again and again. Something new takes a lot more work. It makes our mind work harder to fill new connections. That's why we see the same movies; tell the same stories; listen to the same music. It's hard for the client to take risks, especially if he is not the CEO—he has a job to keep. It's safer to go where everybody else is going.

Our job is about finding a visually interesting way to tell a story. We can categorize innovation in two parts: radical innovation and incremental innovation. Most of the time, we are reshaping things. It's like sampling music. We mix a lot of ideas we see, imagine, or create. Once in a while we find something really new. I'm not sure if in a pure sense this is possible because we all live inside our cultural influences. It's very difficult to find something disconnected to what is happening. Artists, designers, musicians, moviemakers, and writers have always looked for what others were doing. Although this has always happened, we now have the technology that lets us know what everybody is doing on any subject, in quantity and velocity, around the world. We are influenced and inspired by all that is around us. The question is the difference between influence and copy. For example, Picasso got inspired by African art, but he didn't copy it; he interpreted it in a new way.

I work with solutions and ideas for many mediums. I draw a store, a display system, or a book cover thinking the same way. What does this store say to the consumer? How can it be more intelligent? How can I create an emotional connection with the public? How can I materialize the core idea of the brand? We work in a very similar way for editorial design. Of course, there are the technical aspects that come with all platforms.

Shouldn't it just be visual design? Maybe just design? No one in Crama Design Estratégico works alone. Even the client participates when he refuses or approves things, as does the public. Design is teamwork.

We were asked to design a cover solution for a book collection of a famous Brazilian writer, Luis Fernando Verissimo. His writing is about the everyman's day-by-day life, written in a humorous way. Our big challenge was to make about twenty different books, but with a collective identity.

Someone on the team came up with a Woody Allen caricature sculpture. That was when we knew we had it. We knew we should use a sculpture. This 3-D solution would be real and friendly. I ended up creating little sculptures of Verissimo and we put him in various scenarios for each book, and it was a big hit.

Zé Ramalho is a popular Brazilian musician from the Northeast region of Brazil. His music mixes popular and regional singing with pop rock style. This record is a twenty-year anthology, in which he rerecorded his most famous songs with new arrangements. I decided to make a resume of his career showing his regional roots from the popular regional scene.

Zé Ramalho has a very personal style of composing and singing inspired by the folk singers from the Northeast region of Brazil. I felt this album was a very important moment in his career, when he was reprising all his big hits, with different arrangements, mixing all kinds of influences—popular Brazilian music, Indian, some Arabian musical references, and pop rock American and English music from the Beatles, Dylan, and Pink Floyd.

When we had our first conversation, he told me this was a three-album project. The first of the trilogy, *20 Years—Acoustic Anthology*, would be an anthology comprising songs he chose. The second album, *Northeast Nation*, would consist of songs with influences from the Northeast region of Brazil that he had listened to all his life and that had influenced his musical style. In the third album, *Brazil Station*, he would re-create musical influences from composers all over Brazil in a clear reference of a long journey around the country. These three albums were deluxe editions inside boxes with a double CD and a forty-page booklet with writings, photos, and illustrations.

When I started working on the design for the first album, I already had a good idea of what we could do for the other two. Zé Ramalho loves album covers, and I worked closely with him on his. I listened to the recordings and we talked about music and design in the old way of making record covers that is not usual today. It was clear he is a big Beatles fan, and the folk music of Bob Dylan and the magical and surreal covers of Pink Floyd from Hypnosis were always a subject of conversation, as was, of course, his Brazilian roots, where singing is storytelling.

For the first album, 20 Years—Acoustic Anthology, *I wanted to show Zé Ramalho on the cover because it was a twenty-year retrospective and his fans would like to see him. The main idea was to show him with all the musical influences he had behind him. We tried a few alternative cover concepts first.*

For the second album, we were inspired by the Beatles'
Sgt. Pepper's Lonely Hearts Club Band. I knew it would
be a nice opportunity to show his Beatles influence.

*Zé Ramalho's 20 Years—Acoustic Anthology album sold more than a
million copies, and for the cover design we won the Brazilian best album
cover prize. The challenge was how to pull all the elements together.
We decided to make a clean, simple cover because the popular art in
the Northeast region of Brazil is mostly black and white, for economic
reasons. We decided to mix his photographs with the xilo style. For the
title, we made some wood backgrounds and worked in a nice composition.
Inside the booklet, we decided to put a few color photos so that it
would contrast with the black-and-white work.*

*We had a lot of fun finding regional historical celebrities to put in place
of the people on the Sgt. Pepper album. It was a creative game to fill
the scenario with objects, animals, plants, and so on from the Northeast
region of Brazil. In place of the other three Beatles, we picked the
three most important regional popular artists. And inside the booklet
we re-created the famous photo of Paul McCartney on the back of* Sgt.
Pepper *but with Zé Ramalho in the same position. It was a big hit, with
newspapers giving it lots of coverage.*

For the third album, we found inspiration in the title, *Brazil Station*. We wanted to show a big station mixed with the colors of the Brazilian flag, symbolizing his long journey around the country.

The first idea we had for Brazil Station was to put a map with the names of cities substituted with the names of the composers whose songs Zé Ramalho was singing. He didn't like this idea.

After Zé Ramalho rejected the initial direction of the map with the names of the cities, we started working on a graphic solution with the station overprinted with the colors of the Brazilian flag. Even though this was the final album of the trilogy, we did more explorations for this than for any of the others.

31

RODNEY FITCH

HIS SKETCHING HAND IS AN EXTENSION OF HIS LIFE EXPERIENCES.

Rodney Fitch is the founder and chairman of FITCH, the global design agency now owned by WPP. He founded his design practice in 1972, and in 1982, FITCH became the first design business to be listed on the London Stock Exchange as a public company. Rodney's firm has led the design industry for more than three decades with global clients in Europe, the United States, and Asia ranging from architecture and interiors to live events; exhibitions; brand identity; industrial design; and, in particular, retail design. Rodney is also active in the arts, culture, and education. In 2008, he was inaugural design jury president at Cannes and was awarded CBE in 1990 for his influence on the British design industry.

IF YOU CAN'T COMMUNICATE VISUALLY BY DRAWING YOUR IDEA, YOU ARE SERIOUSLY HANDICAPPED AS A DESIGNER.

What some might see as a disadvantage, I see as an advantage. I'm not technologically sound. I don't use technological means for inspiration. The traditional methods have been supplanted by the freedom of information that is available on the Internet. Because it is there and freely available, and people are inherently lazy, they choose that methodology for inspiration. Because of that, what they call inspiration is very often copying or imitation. So, my ignorance doesn't allow me to go there.

What people call a "mood" board, which is inevitably a collection of other people's work, disturbs me. Not only has it become a fact of life for the creators, but the clients have come to expect a kind of shortcut to the ultimate solution.

I am inspired by working with other people. I don't think I could ever work on my own. I enjoy bouncing ideas around. I enjoy the development of ideas and being challenged. I'm inspired by the people I work with; I'm inspired by being alive; I'm inspired by reading; by visiting; and above all, by my own thinking. I spend a good deal of time thinking about projects and possible solutions rather than actually doing the solution. I've heard that some firms make sure there is some thinking time before turning on a computer.

I'm convinced that if you can't communicate visually by drawing your idea, you are seriously handicapped as a designer. One of my great moments of inspiration was a lovely exhibition in London, called "Leonardo, the Designer." The designers of the exhibition had found a wonderful way to take a da Vinci drawing and make a film of how he thought through the drawing. Above each drawing an animated film was projected showing how he thought through the drawing. You felt the thoughts coming down from his brain via his arm, into his pen, as the drawing materialized in front of you. Being able to "draw down" your ideas is a necessity for a designer to produce pure ideas.

Terminal 5 at Heathrow Airport in London called for a radical new image for this large airside duty-free store for Harrods.

One of my favorite projects is called "Great in Hong Kong." What was most challenging was that this was a first for Hong Kong—it's a 37,674 sq. ft (3,500 m²) upscale food court and supermarket in a shopping mall. We did a play on the name, GREAT, for the signage, identity, packaging, and so on. This project was challenging from the point of view of budget, space, and time.

The project was an attempt at some kind of counterculture. Nearly all of the traditional markets you would visit in China are very confusing. There is no clarity. They work on the assumption that, given the nature of Chinese shopping habits, where you might go to the market twice a day, you would know where to go for fish or meat. But to a stranger, they are completely nonnavigable and confusing.

A subject close to my heart is specialism. For example, if you go to Harvard Business School, you will become a businessman; if you go to an art school, you will become an artist or a graphic designer or an interior designer; if you go to a traditional university and study history or English, however, it isn't assumed that you will become a historian or an English teacher or a writer.

There is a separation of education, for either education's sake or vocationally for a career. Today's education is driving students increasingly toward specialties so that when they emerge from design school they specialize as a graphic designer or an environmental designer. There's nothing wrong with that, but the antidote is that our graduates need to be able to work collaboratively when they come out of school. Many aren't taught in school that the object of the exercise is to work as part of a team, and that this team will collectively solve that task or challenge with all the skills you have. Just because you studied packaging doesn't mean you will do only packaging. You need designers who do more and more collaborative work. If you're just a packaging design

firm you need to find a way of collaborating with other businesses so that you can provide a more holistic solution. Or if you're a small firm that works across disciplines, your designers from the different disciplines need to work together.

This is a necessity if you want to work with major global clients. I set up FITCH in this model. In the FITCH business we are multidisciplinary in our studios. We also work collaboratively across our studios with a selection of disciplines. That's good for us and good for our clients.

32

DESIGNER
LOS ANGELES, CA, USA

GORDON THOMPSON III

IS A DEMOCRATIC DESIGNER.

After ten years at Nike, where he was global creative director overseeing the design and creation of retail, multimedia, apparel, footwear, and equipment design worldwide, Gordon Thompson III went to Cole Haan as executive vice president and creative director, innovating and introducing Nike Air technology in the fashion world. He left in 2007, and is now a creative consultant to brands such as Disney, Lilly Pulitzer, and Reyn Spooner.

WHEN I HAVE A DESIGN PROBLEM TO SOLVE, MY EYES BECOME MUCH WIDER.

I grew up in southern California, and my parents took me to Disneyland all the time. I was fascinated with the Disneyland environment. It was complete escapism, yet everything was completely designed. Of course, at the time I didn't realize that. But something came to life there, and I loved the idea of creating a place where people went away and were entrenched in it. Even today, it's amazing to get behind the scenes of how the park was created and how it works.

My training is unique, in that I got my undergraduate degree in architecture at the University of Southern California. Five years of architectural history gives you a good basis for referencing and conjuring up ideas. I coupled that with a graduate degree from the Art Center College of Design, in Pasadena, California, which is all about environment design, including hospitality, set, and costume design. I learned a lot about conceptual design, such as how to follow a script, concept, or strategy.

I had two weird bookends that made me look at inspiration in different ways. When I arrived at Nike, with my first project being Niketown, I was told, "We just need a store." The strategy was something like, "We want to immerse the athlete in a great place, we want to show all the product, we want to show that we care as much about tennis as we do about running, we want to show retailers that we're bigger than just a couple of sneakers—and we want to push the connection between athletes and the product." Because the program kept expanding, the design needed to include an organizing principle.

When I was a sketch artist at Warner Bros., I was working on *Back to the Future*. The script had a street-organizing principle where it always went back to the town square. So, when I was working on Niketown, I used the organizing principle of a city or a community, but a community of sport. With this background of a controlled environment, you can take the consumer or athlete off the street and into a world that's completely immersed in sports. That world is full of archives, merchandise, and storytelling. I think we learned a lot from the first store in how to move people through and how to sell the product within the store. At the time, this idea was pretty new. No one had really done retail theatre like this before.

Inspiration comes to me from having a problem to solve. I can't really just walk down the street and say, "Oh, that's inspiring." I think more like an architect. I have to be presented with something: "We have this problem; we need you to figure out how we can solve it or make it less of a problem."

When I have a problem to solve, my eyes become much wider. For instance, a shoe store has a lot of back stock. I knew that, of course, but I had never really thought about it. So, I didn't really know what the back of a shoe store looked like. But with Niketown, I had a problem to solve. You have all these boxes, and somehow you have to get them to the main floor, your selling floor. Real estate is very expensive in cities, so typically you want to put your shoe storage on another floor, but how do you do that so that the customer doesn't walk away?

Late one night, I was watching *The Jetsons*. I looked at the tube that George comes through from his home to his office, and I thought, that's a really interesting idea. I've always loved the plastic bank deposit tubes that use air pressure to send, say, your check to some "magical place" in the bank, and then send you the cash in return. I think it's the fantasy of it, again going back to Disneyland. Things just sort of appear, and I love that.

I wouldn't have had the idea of delivering shoes in a tube if I had not been watching The Jetsons. *It would not have crystallized in my mind that using a pneumatic tube to move product from one place to another would be iconic and unique for Nike. That's where the shoe tube idea originated.*

CUT # OF TUBES AND USE DUMB WAITERS AS BACK-UP.

EXPOSE IN PLAN IN EXTERIOR OF BLDGS LIKE PLIGHT AND FORCE. (PLAT DOOR).

SHOE TUBE DOWN

For Niketown, it was important for us to highlight the brand first and then the product. So, if you walked in and were immersed in what Nike stood for as a brand, when you encountered the product it would make more sense.

Inspiration is based more on a problem that needs to be solved. I start really thinking about, "What if it looked like this? What if it featured this?" I find art inspiring. I find architecture inspiring, but it becomes more real to me when there's a problem to solve or when there's an actual thing to apply.

For architecture, you have a program. There are so many rooms; there's so much square footage; it has to be so tall. You have parameters to work with. Then it's the designer's job to take those parameters and bring them to life, and sometimes push back. I think more like a true designer where I like to show that I solved this problem. I like to prove my theories or my inspirations against something that's happened in history. If it worked back then, the modern version of that could work as well.

The concept of not having product on the main floor really took people by surprise. It was a very different way of looking at retail. It's almost like inverting the typical retail store where you put all the products by the door. You had to actually go through a door, and then you had to go through another door to even see a shoe.

I consciously decided that the Niketown stores should not be perfectly square. Instead, they should feature a lot of architectural randomness. They provide more of a wandering type of experience. You leave one pavilion and go to the next one. That was very World's Fair–oriented because it's more of an American idea to ramble where you wander and discover.

When I was at Cole Haan, we practiced the three *I*'s: innovation, ideation, and inspiration. How do you guide a customer through a process of education, with the final conclusion being "does the shoe work for me, does it fit, and will I buy it?"

I learned that when you give people something they didn't expect, they like it much more. They have an affinity for newness and for rethinking something. It gave me enormous confidence in doing all of the other projects I did at Nike, because I knew that was the right road. Whether it's innovation in a product or innovation in a store design, it gets people excited and endears them to you.

I think there are designers who give the client what they want, and they'll be good staff designers. Design stars are the ones who lead, who really rethink the problem, apply what they learned in design school (and what they hopefully have in their DNA), and look at a problem from a different angle.

For the Niketown pavilions, there was a central circulation path through the town square, and then there was a secondary path that connected the pavilions together, so you didn't have to always go back to the town square to move from one pavilion to the next.

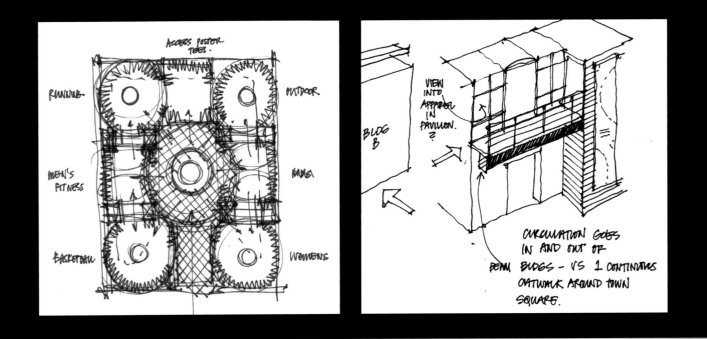

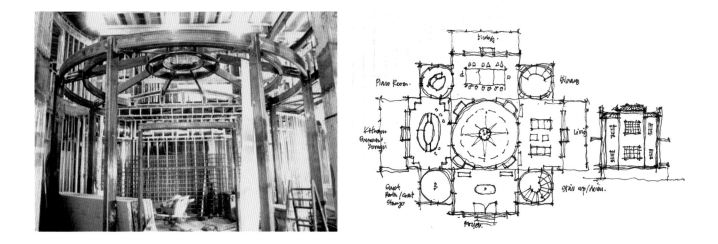

Typically in department stores, cosmetics are on the first floor—you always walk through the cosmetics area before you reach your destination. I thought, what would happen if you didn't have anything on the main floor, and everything was tucked in these pavilions, like a shopping street of sports. You interact with people on that street; you shop in these pavilions where you're close to the product. It's a way to separate the circulation from the actual shopping. It's also a way to create a community, a personality, and a conversation area in the stores.

I am inspired by taking something from one style of business or product and applying it to a completely different product. At Nike, that was the DNA for footwear design. Cars, guitars, you name it; it all could be extrapolated and put into a shoe, apparel, or equipment.

That's where design leadership exists: in being able to look at something differently, and understand that a little detail on a car could make a fantastic detail on a shoe. Sometimes, it is as simple as that.

The best designers are the ones with their eyes wide open. It's impossible to be a Republican designer. I just don't think they exist in America. You have to be extremely democratic. Everything is design inspiration.

Building brands is not for the faint of heart. I think you have to have a lot of dedication to what you're doing. it's not easy, and it's a lot of work. It happens daily. You can't take a break. You have to be constantly innovating, coming up with new ideas, keeping the consumer engaged, rethinking what you did, moving forward, being relevant.

THE RESOLUTION REDUX

AS DESIGNERS, WE ARE BLESSED WITH THE ABILITY TO STIR EMOTION AND ACTION WITH THE RESULTS OF OUR WORK. LET'S USE OUR STRATEGIC AND VISUAL POWERS TO ENGENDER PASSION FOR OURSELVES AND EMOTION IN OTHERS.

DON'T BE AFRAID TO FAIL. If we don't try, we'll never know. Designers such as Derek Welch and his partner Jason Bacon take risks because they are feeding their passions. If design nirvana can be described as doing for a living what we would do in our leisure time for free, those willing to take a chance are those who will be rewarded.

THINK MORE, WRITE MORE. I keep meaning to take the time to ponder. And I'm always threatening to finish a book or two that I've started. William Drenttel and Jessica Helfand are thinking designers. Study their prolific output. Read about design. Write about design. It will stimulate your creative lobes in a new way that solely "visual in, visual out" won't.

LIVE YOUR PASSION. Dora Drimalas and Brian Flynn infuse their lives with their passion for design. With a "why not?" attitude and a skilled sense of design, you can turn your personal interests into solutions, designs, and business opportunities that will, in turn, continue to feed and grow your passions.

WE CREATE EXPERIENCES. As Joe Duffy showed us, designers should not be item designers, we should be experience designers. Even when we are creating one piece of the experience, we need to be aware of how it fits into the whole story. Consumers judge by the combined brand touch points they encounter.

SIMPLE IS STRONG. The simple solutions Louk de Sévaux came up with reminds me that, many times, the most powerful solutions are the simplest. The fact that it takes so long to get to that simple design truth is one of our challenges as designers. Maybe it's just that it takes that long to strip away all the "decoration" that never needed to be there in the first place.

CREATE THE FUTURE. Ricardo Leite reminds us that people gravitate toward what they know. But we have the platform as designers to give the consumer (and often our clients) something they don't know they need yet. That's when design transcends and shows what it's really made of.

DESIGN IS SIMPLY BEAUTIFUL. As Rodney Fitch sketches the future, we have the power as designers to take the spark of an idea and sketch that spark until it responds and grows into a simple, sophisticated solution that can bring everyday joy to a consumer.

MAKE CONNECTIONS. We all have unique experiences embedded in our brains. Seeing how Gordon Thompson made the leap from *The Jetsons* to the Niketown shoe tube reminds us to mine what we already have inside us. By remembering those internal connections and viewing the world with "wider eyes," we will encounter design solutions unexpectedly.

CONTRIBUTOR INDEX

Ronald Kapaz // 183
Oz Design
Horacio Lafer, 671
São Paulo SP
Brazil 04537-083
www.ozdesign.com.br
55.11.30731769

Ricardo Leite // 229
Crama Design Estratégico
RuaA Marquês de São Vicente
22/302
Rio de Janeiro, Brazil
22451-040
www.crama.com.br
55.212.5128555

Joel Nakamura // 91
72 Bobcat Trail
Santa Fe, NM 87505 USA
www.joelnakamura.com
505.989.1404

Agnete Oernsholt // 83
OERNSHOLT
2301 Castilian Drive
Los Angeles, CA 90068 USA
www.oernsholt.com
310.804.1480

Dario Robleto // 177
San Antonio, TX USA

Lorenzo Shakespear // 105
Shakespear Design
Dardo Rocha 2754
Martinez (1640)
Buenos Aires, Argentina
www.shakespearweb.com
54.114.8361333

Christopher Simmons // 47
MINE
190 Putnam St.
San Francisco, CA 94110 USA
www.minesf.com
415.647.MINE (6463)

Fiodor Sumkin // 125
Opera 78
18 rue de Berne
75008 Paris, France
www.opera78.com
33.6.98.45.24.89

Gordon Thompson III // 243
Los Angeles, CA USA

Lane Twitchell // 151
Lane Twitchell Studio
216 Lincoln Pl. #61
Brooklyn, NY 11217 USA
718.916.2057

Michael Vanderbyl // 165
Vanderbyl Design
171 Second St., Second Floor
San Francisco, CA 94105 USA
www.vanderbyldesign.com
415.543.8447

Fumi Watanabe // 143
4633 45th Ave., S
Seattle, WA 98118 USA
www.alkemidesign.com
206.313.9545

Derek Welch // 193
UNKL
600 NW Naito Pkwy., Suite F
Portland, OR 97209 USA
www.big-giant.com
503.221.1079

Ann Willoughby // 135
Willoughby Design Group
602 Westport Road
Kansas City, MO 64111 USA
www.willoughbydesign.com
816.561.4189

Wang Xu // 119
Guangdong Museum of Art
No. 38 Yanyu Road
Er-sha Island
Guangzhou, China 510105
www.wx-design.com
86.20.87351951

ABOUT THE AUTHOR

After growing up in Murray, a small Kentucky town located between Possum Trot and Monkey's Eyebrow, Stanley Hainsworth worked as an actor for several years before landing in the design profession, where he is still free to pursue multiple facial hair options. For the next twenty years, Hainsworth was creative director at Nike, LEGO, and Starbucks before forming his own creative agency, Tether. Located in Seattle, Washington, Tether is an agency, a retail store, and an art gallery that works with numerous brands across the design disciplines. Tether also births their own brands, believing that designers are problem solvers who know how to create stories that consumers will want to connect with.

Along his design journey, Hainsworth has learned and been inspired from all the amazing designers he has worked with over the years and is honored to have them participate in this book.